Language BOOSTERS

Written by
Collene Dobelmann and Amy Stern

Editors: Maria Gallardo, MA/Gillan Snoddy
Illustrator: Jenny Campbell
Cover Illustrator: Rick Grayson
Designer/Production: Alicia Schulte
Art Director: Moonhee Pak
Project Director: Stacey Faulkner

Copyright © 2009 Creative Teaching Press Inc., Huntington Beach, CA 92649
Reproduction of activities in any manner for use in the classroom and not for commercial sale is permissible.
Reproduction of these materials for an entire school or for a school system is strictly prohibited.

Table of Contents

Introduction 3–5
How to Use This Book 6

Hello and Goodbye 7
The First Day of School 8
In My Classroom 9
School Supplies 10
People in School 11
The Playground 12
School Rules 13
Colors 14
Numbers 15
The Days of the Week 16
The Months of the Year 17
The Four Seasons 18
Winter 19
Spring 20
Summer 21
Autumn 22
My Body 23
Staying Healthy 24
The Five Senses 25
Jose's Family 26
Aunts and Uncles 27
Grandparents 28
At Home 29
In the Kitchen 30
In the Bathroom 31
Clean It Up! 32
Time to Eat 33
Time for Bed 34
Manners 35
Helping Others 36
Clothes 37
Shopping for Clothes 38
Fruit and Vegetables 39
Other Foods 40
Shopping for Food 41
Going to a Restaurant 42
Our Neighborhood 43
Community Helpers 44
Transportation 45
The Airport 46
The Library 47
The Post Office 48
The Hospital 49
The Fire Station 50
Math Time 51
Shapes 52
Money 53
Measurement 54
Homework 55
Computers 56

Time to Play 57
A Day at the Beach 58
A Day at the Park 59
A Day at the Pool 60
A Day at the Fair 61
Cats 62
Dogs 63
Rabbits and Hamsters 64
Jump Rope 65
Tag 66
Kickball 67
Music 68
Art 69
Dance 70
Geography 71
Birthdays 72
Happy New Year! 73
Valentine's Day 74
Easter 75
Fourth of July 76
Halloween 77
Veterans Day 78
Christmas 79
Chanukah 80
Kwanzaa 81
Plants 82
Nonliving Things 83
Habitats 84
Desert Life 85
Ocean Life 86
Mountain Life 87
Rain Forest Life 88
Let's Recycle 89
Endangered Animals 90
Our Earth 91
Weather 92
Electricity 93
Night Sky 94
Dinosaurs 95
Rocks 96
Life Cycle of a Butterfly 97
Insects 98
Spiders 99
The Statue of Liberty 100
Benjamin Franklin 101
Abraham Lincoln 102
Harriet Tubman 103
Helen Keller 104
Amelia Earhart 105
Sally Ride 106

Answer Key 107–111
Language Proficiency Reference Chart 112

Introduction

Language Boosters provides 100 practice pages designed to support students' language proficiency through repeated exposure to fundamental components of language instruction, including vocabulary, word usage, comprehension, multiple meaning words, and cognitive and written language. In addition, practice pages focus on common academic content themes to aid cross-curricular learning and align with language arts, math, science, and social studies curricula.

Research-Based Instruction and the Importance of Language Proficiency

As research has shown, word knowledge is the bridge to reading success and a key predictor of overall achievement in school. *Language Boosters* provides expert instruction in mastering the fundamentals of language proficiency to help all students develop the understanding and confidence necessary to learn the English language.

In addition, *Language Boosters* features word-building strategies that target intentional and systematic vocabulary instruction designed around meaningful everyday and academic topics. This research-based format is recognized as especially effective for English Language Learners who are not exposed to rich sources of word knowledge and indirect learning.

Support for English Language Learners

State standards require all students, regardless of language proficiency levels, to meet academic content standards. *Language Boosters* guides students toward meeting those challenging standards in the second-grade classroom and is geared for students who have reached an intermediate level of language proficiency.

While all students will benefit from repeated practice with the language skills and content themes presented, *Language Boosters* offers a variety of features to specifically support your English Language Learners. The 100 practice pages are presented in progressive order; align with language arts, math, science, and social studies curricula; and are based on the most current proficiency standards for English Language Development (see reference chart on page 112). Each practice page features repetition and predictability of skills and tasks through consistent wording of directions, repeating question formats, simple sentence structure, and numerous illustrations for strong visual reference.

Introduction **3**

Practice Pages
The five questions on each practice page follow the same consistent format:

1. Vocabulary—everyday and academic words

2. Word Usage—grammar, syntax, mechanics, and other language conventions

3. Comprehension—context clues, word meaning, recall, and making inferences

4. Synonyms, Antonyms, and Multiple-Meaning Words—homographs and homophones

5. Cognitive and Written Language—responses to language, including personal connections

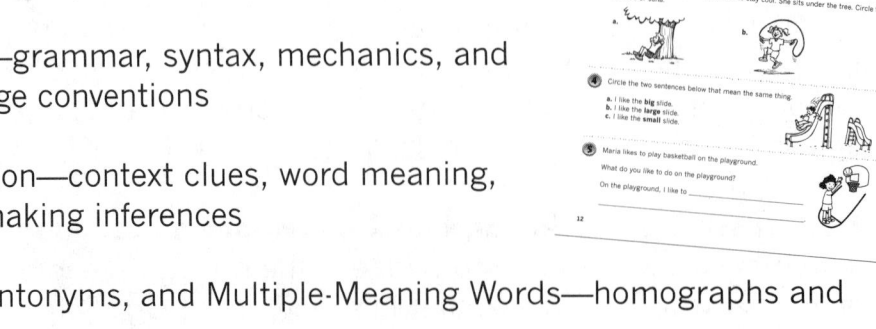

Vocabulary
These are specifically targeted words that students encounter in everyday (social) and curriculum-related (academic) settings. Academic vocabulary is more difficult to master because it is generally not specifically taught or used outside the classroom and draws on new vocabulary not typically encountered in everyday settings.

manners
family
nocturnal
sphere

For additional learning support, *Language Boosters* provides a two-step scaffolding strategy to introduce academic vocabulary while building content knowledge. When introduced the first time, each academic vocabulary word appears in **boldface** with its definition. When presented the second time, the word usually appears with a definition prompt. When used subsequently, it appears without any additional support.

My apple _____ green.
    is   am

Word Usage
It is important for all students to understand and practice the often complex rules that govern the English language, such as sentence word order and necessary grammar and spelling rules. In addition to supporting questions in this category with helpful illustrations for visual reference, *Language Boosters* features short and simple sentences so as not to overwhelm the English Language Learner.

Introduction

Comprehension

Exposure to and use of words in numerous contexts promotes word learning and reading comprehension. To support the English Language Learner, *Language Boosters* features simple sentence structure and strong picture and language clues for questions in this category to help students gather meaning from words within context and to reinforce comprehension.

Mara goes to P.E. on Monday. She goes to music class on Tuesday.

Mara goes to _____ on Wednesday.
              P.E.   music class

Synonyms, Antonyms, and Multiple-Meaning Words

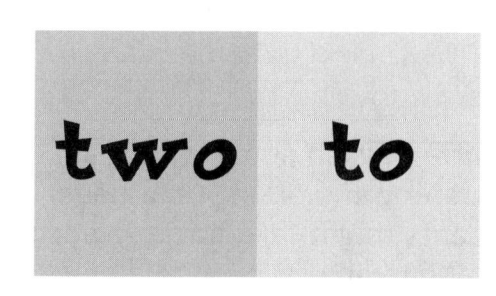

It is important for all students to understand the need for using words that provide dimension, clarity, precision, and enrichment in the English language. This is particularly true for the English Language Learner, who may be relying on a limited amount of word knowledge to convey meanings or ideas. When describing a friend, for example, learning synonyms for the word *nice* enables students to describe more specific characteristics, such *kind*, *happy*, and *friendly*.

Cognitive and Written Language

A student's cognitive language typically exceeds his or her ability to produce oral or written language. This is especially true for English Language Learners, who may comprehend far more than the limited English that they are able to produce. It is important to provide students with multiple opportunities to interact with and respond to words and picture clues in a variety of ways to develop cognitive and written language proficiency. Consequently, the last question on each *Language Boosters* practice page features cognitive and written-language opportunities, such as identifying rhyming words, sequencing events, alphabetizing words, or responding to open-ended questions.

a. ___last___    b. ___first___    c. ___next___

Introduction 5

How to Use This Book

Use *Language Boosters* as a supplement to your English Language Arts or English Language Development curriculums to accentuate learning for both native English speakers and English Language Learners. Use the pages in order of appearance to make the most of the built-in scaffolding for the introduction of vocabulary, skills, and tasks. Or choose pages that fit with current themes or topics of study. Please note that students completing pages out of order may need additional instructional support. Present the practice pages using any of the instructional methods suggested below to aid in the development of listening, speaking, reading, and writing skills.

Individual Work
Depending on the ability levels of your students, have them complete pages individually for additional reinforcement with language skills or have them use pages together with guidance from a teacher or teaching assistant to work through the problems at a comfortable pace.

Paired Learning
Pairing students of differing ability levels or pairing a native English speaker with an English Language Learner can be an effective learning strategy. If working on a page such as Time to Play (page 57) or Plants (page 82), students might take turns saying the names of objects on each page or finding antonyms. When one student gets stuck, his or her partner is there to lend support.

Small Group Activities
It has been found that language learners working in groups (cooperative learning) will achieve more, retain more in long-term memory, and use higher-level reasoning strategies more frequently when they learn information cooperatively.

Have students working in groups of five each take responsibility for one of the questions on each page, sharing answers with group mates, and consulting each other when stuck on a question. Small groups might also work clockwise in a circle, stating the names of objects presented on a page, or answering questions such as, "What fruits do you like?" (page 39) or "What do you like to do at the beach?" (page 58).

Large Group Activities
Present large-group lessons using a transparency, document camera, or scanned practice page for use with your interactive white board to work through problems together with the class. Incorporate total physical response (TPR), a technique by which students demonstrate comprehension and answer questions through physical motions. Giving a "thumbs-up" or standing up might represent a *yes* answer, while "thumbs-down" or sitting down might represent a *no* answer. For example, when learning about clothing (page 37) you might point or call out items on the page and say *Stand up if this is summer clothing* or *Sit down if this is winter clothing*.

Name _____ Date _____

Hello and Goodbye

1 I greet my friends when I see them. I greet my teacher in the morning. When you greet someone, you say:

a. hello

b. goodbye

2 Our teacher _____ nice.
    is   are

She always says, "Good morning, class."

3 It is the end of the day. It is time to go home. What do you say to your friends?

a. Hi

b. Bye

4 Draw a line from each sentence to the correct picture.

1. Amy waves to her friends.   **a.**

2. The ocean has big waves.   **b.**

5 Write two other ways to say hello and goodbye.

Hello _____   _____

Goodbye _____   _____

The First Day of School

1. There are many rules at school. Here is one rule at school: Wait for your turn to talk. A *rule* is:

  a. a direction you must follow

  b. a direction you do not follow

2. Sarah has two best _____ at school.
  friend   friends

3. Max cried on the first day of school. How did he feel?

  a. sad

  b. happy

4. Find a word in Sentence A that means the same as a word in Sentence B. Circle the two words.

  A. I am happy on the first day of school.
  B. I am glad to see my friends.

5. Write the name of someone who sits next to you in class.

_____

Name _____ Date _____

In My Classroom

1. The students lined up in a straight row at the door. Circle the picture that shows a row.

a.    b.

2. Circle the name of a person in the sentence below:

Carmen works at her desk.

3. Lisa's class has a pet turtle. She likes to feel its hard shell. Circle the picture of the students' pet.

a.    b.

4. The students are quiet today. The opposite of *quiet* is:

a. silent   **b.** loud

5. Circle two words that rhyme with *clock*.

bag    block    sock    flag

Name   Date

School Supplies

1. Martin loves to color with crayons. Circle the picture that shows Martin.

a.

b.

2. Jenny and Regina are friends.

_____ read books together.
We   They

3. Angel is doing his art project. His fingers are sticky. What is Angel using?

a. glue

b. scissors

4. Find a word in Sentence A that sounds like a word in Sentence B. Circle the two words.

A. I always write with a pencil.

B. He kicked with his right foot.

5. Circle two things you use at school.

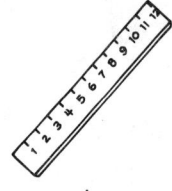

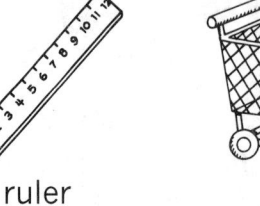

ruler   cart   paper   rake

Name _____   Date _____

People in School

1. Complete the sentence below. Ms. Hong teaches us math.

Ms. Hong is our _____.

a.

teacher

b.

bus driver

2. Rewrite the sentence below correctly. Find one missing capital letter and one missing period.

the nurse helps students who are sick

_____

3. The librarian helps students find good books. Circle the picture that shows the librarian.

a.

b.

4. The student works at his desk.

He sits _____ his chair.
        on   off

5. Write the name of your teacher.

_____

11

Name _____   Date _____

The Playground

1 It is a rainy day. The playground is wet. Circle the picture that shows a wet playground.

a.   b.

2 We are on the playground.

_____ race Raul to the swings.
I   Me

3 It is hot on the playground. Jena likes to stay cool. She sits under the tree. Circle the picture of Jena.

a.   b.

4 Circle the two sentences below that mean the same thing.

   a. I like the big slide.
   b. I like the large slide.
   c. I like the small slide.

5 Maria likes to play basketball on the playground.

What do you like to do on the playground?

On the playground, I like to _____

_____.

Name _____   Date _____

School Rules

1 We have to walk in a straight line. We have to follow one behind the other. Circle the picture that shows a straight line.

a.   b.

2 Walk in the hall. Do not run.

This is a _____ at my school.
         rule   rules

3 Our teacher tells us to raise our hands before we speak. Circle the picture of the student following this rule.

a.   b.

4 Circle the two sentences that mean the same thing.

   a. Friends are nice to each other.
   b. Friends are mean to each other.
   c. Friends are kind to each other.

5 We have to do our homework in a notebook. The two words *home* and *work* make up the word *homework*. What two words make up the word *notebook*?

home + work = homework

_____ + _____ = notebook

13

Name _____   Date _____

Colors

1. The sky is blue. Circle two choices below that can be blue.

   a.  sun   b.  bird   c. 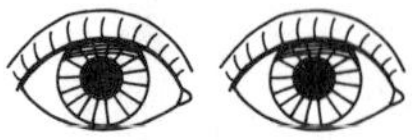 eyes   d.  grapes

2. My apple _____ green.
   is   am

3. Mandy has a white dog. It has black spots. Circle the picture of Mandy's dog.

   a.    b.

4. Find a word in Sentence A that sounds like a word in Sentence B. Circle the two words.

   A. The red rose is pretty.   B. Yesterday I read a book.

5. Color the stars with two colors you like. Then finish the sentence below.

   I like the colors _____ and _____.

Name Date

Numbers

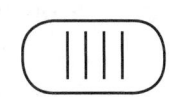

1 I see _____ fish in a bowl.

a. two b. three c. four

2 Rewrite the sentence below correctly. Find one missing capital letter and one missing period.

molly is five years old

_____

3 Jim saves his money. He wants to buy a new toy. Jim has three coins. Circle the picture that shows Jim's coins.

a.  b.

4 Find a word in Sentence A that sounds like a word in Sentence B. Circle the two words.

A. I ride the bus to school.

B. I have two scoops of ice cream.

5 Circle two words that rhyme with *three*.

toe  tree  tail  key

Name _____   Date _____

The Days of the Week

1 A day is a measure of time. There are seven days in a week. Circle the day after Tuesday. Put an X over the day before Monday.

Sunday   Monday   Tuesday   Wednesday

Thursday   Friday   Saturday

2 Rewrite the sentence below correctly. Find one missing capital letter and one missing period.

My family eats pizza every friday

_____

3 Mara goes to P.E. on Monday. She goes to music class on Tuesday.

Mara goes to _____ on Wednesday.
               P.E.   music class

4 *First* and *last* are opposites. Complete each sentence with the correct word.

1. The _____ day of the school week is Monday.
       first   last

2. The _____ day of the school week is Friday.
       first   last

5 Look at the names of the days of the week below.

Sunday   Monday   Tuesday   Wednesday   Thursday   Friday   Saturday

What small word is at the end of each name? _____

Name _____ Date _____

The Months of the Year

1 We circled the date of the party on the calendar. Write the date on the line below.

_____

2 There are 12 _____ in one year.
                  month   months

3 January is a cold month. We wear jackets and gloves. July is a hot month. We wear shorts and T-shirts. Circle the picture that shows January. Put an X over the picture that shows July.

a.

b.

4 Draw a line from each sentence to the correct picture.

a.

1. I like to march with the band.

2. My birthday is in March.

b.

5 Complete the sentence below with the correct month.

I was born in the month of _____.

Name _____ Date _____

The Four Seasons

1 A season is a time of year. Circle your favorite season.

winter    spring    summer    fall

2 Circle the name of a person in this sentence:

Miguel starts school in the fall.

3 Marlena goes to the beach every day. She swims in the ocean. She plays in the sand. Circle the picture that shows this season.

a.    b.

4 Circle the two sentences below that mean the same thing.

a. The leaves blow off the trees in the fall.
b. The leaves blow off the trees in autumn.
c. The leaves blow off the trees in spring.

5 A **compound word** is a word made of two smaller words. Write compound words for three things you might see in winter.

snow + storm = snowstorm

snow + man    snow + ball 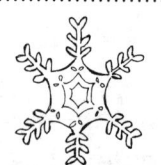   snow + flake

_____   _____   _____

18

Name _____ Date _____

Winter

1. My favorite season is winter. The weather is cold. We play in the snow. Circle the picture that shows winter weather.

a.    b.

2. Raquel _____ a warm coat.
         have   has

She _____ it in the winter.
    wear   wears

3. Jorge jumped up out of bed and looked outside. "I can build a snowman today!" he exclaimed. What did Jorge see when he looked outside?

a. snow   b. rain

4. The winter weather is too cold for me.

Another word for *cold* is:

a. chilly   b. warm

5. Skiing is a popular winter sport. A lot of people ski during winter. Circle the pictures of two more sports that are popular during winter.

snowboarding    tennis 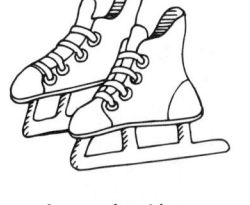   ice skating    golfing

Language Boosters • Gr. 2 © 2009 Creative Teaching Press

19

Name _____   Date _____

Spring

1 The Ross family owns a big farm. Many of their animals give birth in the spring. The cows have calves, the pigs have piglets, and the ducks have ducklings. In the sentence above, *give birth* means:

   a. to live on a farm
   b. to have babies

---

2 Our rabbit Fluffy had three _____ in April.

   bunny   bunnies

---

3 Mr. Sanchez planted seeds in his garden. He waters the seeds every day. They get a lot of sunshine. What will happen next?

   a. He will plant more seeds.
   b. A plant will grow.

---

4 Find a word in Sentence A that sounds like a word in Sentence B. Circle the two words.

   A. Mom likes the sweet, flowery scent of roses.

   B. We sent her a birthday card.

---

5 Spring is a nice time to be outdoors. Many families go to parks and have picnics. Complete the sentence below.

   During spring, I like to _____
   _____

20

Name _____   Date _____

Summer

1 Frank lives in the city. The air gets very humid in the summer. Frank sweats a lot. On a humid day, Frank feels:

   a. cool and fresh   **b.** hot and moist

2 We go on vacation every summer.

   Last year we _____ to Florida.
   <u>flew   flies</u>

3 Summer is Valerie's favorite time of year. She gets a break from school. She plays outside with her friends. Circle one more reason why Valerie might like summer so much.

   a. She rides her bike every day.   **b.** She has a lot of homework.

4 Find a word in Sentence A that means the opposite of a word in Sentence B. Circle the two words.

   A. The sun burns my skin.   **B.** The snow freezes the spring flowers.

5 Judy swims in her pool every day. Circle two words that rhyme with *pool*.

   pail    school    stool    bowl

21

Name _____   Date _____

Autumn

1. Autumn is a special time of year for Kate's family. They all get together at Kate's house for a Thanksgiving celebration. In the sentence above, *celebration* means:

   a. a special event or holiday
   b. something that happens every day

2. The leaves on our trees will change colors in autumn. They will turn yellow, orange, and red. They will fall off the trees. Another way to write *they will* is:

   a. they're   **b.** they'll

3. Autumn is also called fall. Autumn is the season between summer and winter. Many children go back to school in September. The weather gets cooler. Which of the following is true about autumn?

   a. October and November are months in autumn.
   b. Autumn is the hottest season of the year.

4. Circle the two sentences below that use the word *patch* in the same way.

   a. We got a big pumpkin at the pumpkin patch. 
   b. My mom put a patch over the hole on my pants. 
   c. The vegetable patch is full of fresh corn.

5. Jessica's mom is baking an apple pie for dessert. First, she cut up the apples. Next, she put the apples in the pan. Last, she put the pie in the oven. Write the words *first*, *next*, and *last* under the correct pictures.

   a.  _____   **b.**  _____   **c.** _____

Name _____   Date _____

My Body

1 Your face has one nose, one mouth, and two _____.

   a. hands   **b.** eyes   **c.** elbows

2 A **verb** is an action word that tells what someone or something does. Circle the verb in the sentence below:

   Frank runs very fast.

3 Samantha has a tummy ache. She goes to the school nurse. What part of Samantha's body hurts?

   a. arm   **b.** back   **c.** stomach

4 Your head is at the top of your body. Your feet are at the opposite end.

   They are at the _____ of your body.

   a. bottom   **b.** middle

5 Circle the words that name parts of your body.

   tail    ear 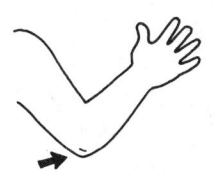   elbow    wing    toes

23

Name _____   Date _____

Staying Healthy

1 Fruit is good for you. Apples and bananas are healthy snacks. In the sentence above, the word *healthy* means:

   a. bad for your body

   b. good for your body

2 My brother and I go to the doctor every year.

   _____ both go to Dr. Martinez.
   He   We

3 Exercise is good for your heart. It helps you grow strong. I get exercise when I run and jump rope. Circle the picture that shows a person who is exercising.

   a.   b.

4 Find a word in Sentence A that means the opposite of a word in Sentence B. Circle the two words.

   A. Vitamins help your body stay strong.
   B. The illness made him weak.

5 You brush your teeth with a toothbrush.

   You brush your _____ with a hairbrush.

24

Name _____ Date _____

The Five Senses

1 The five senses are touch, taste, sight, smell, and hearing. Circle the two pictures of the people who are using the same sense.

a.   b.   c.

---

2 A **complete sentence** is a group of words that tells a complete idea. It begins with a capital letter and ends with a period (.), question mark (?), or exclamation mark (!). Circle the complete sentence.

a. Kevin smelled the apple pie.
b. smelled the apple pie

---

3 We use our five senses to feel, taste, see, smell, and hear. We feel with our hands, and we taste with our tongues. Write *see*, *smell*, and *hear* on the lines next to the body parts we use for these senses.

---

4 Choose one of the words below to correctly complete both sentences.

a. sound   b. taste   c. sight

Yvonne loves the _____ of fresh baked bread.

My sister has great _____ in clothes.

---

5 Matt finished his homework without help. He said, "That was a piece of cake." This means that:

a. Matt's homework was cake.
b. Matt's homework was easy.

25

Name   Date

Jose's Family

1. Jose has a nice family. He has a mother, a father, and one sister. A family is a group of people who are related to each other and live together. Circle the picture that shows a family.

   a.    b.

2. Circle the word that describes how Jose feels.

   Jose is sad that his train is broken.

3. Jose's father fights fires. He climbs up a long ladder. He uses a water hose. Circle the picture of Jose's father.

   a.    b.

4. Find a word in Sentence A that sounds the same as a word in Sentence B. Circle the two words.

   A. Mr. Ramos has a son.

   B. Jose wears a hat in the sun.

5. Jose and his family have a pet snake. Circle three words that rhyme with *snake*.

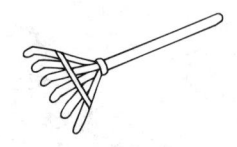

   rake    steak    lake 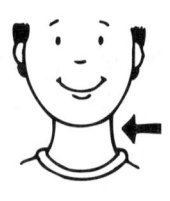   neck

26

Name _____ Date _____

Aunts and Uncles

1 My mom has a sister. She is my _____.
$\quad\quad\quad\quad\quad\quad\quad\quad\quad\quad\quad\quad\quad\quad\quad\quad$ aunt $\quad\quad$ uncle

$\quad$ My aunt's husband is my _____.
$\quad\quad\quad\quad\quad\quad\quad\quad\quad\quad\quad\quad\quad\quad\quad$ aunt $\quad\quad$ uncle

2 I _____ fun with Uncle Jesse.
$\quad\quad$ has $\quad\quad$ have

$\quad$ He always _____ football with me.
$\quad\quad\quad\quad\quad\quad\quad\quad$ play $\quad\quad$ plays

3 Aunt Gloria and Uncle Jesse have a son named Alfred.

$\quad$ Alfred is my _____.

$\quad$ **a.** cousin $\quad\quad\quad$ **b.** sister

4 Circle the two words in the sentence below that sound the same.

$\quad$ My aunt saw an ant on the picnic table.

5 These words are in ABC order:
dad, mom, son

When putting words in ABC order, look at the first letter of each word to help you. Write the following three words in ABC order on the lines below:
aunt, uncle, cousin

_____   _____   _____

27

Name   Date

Grandparents

1 Marcos visits his grandparents in Mexico every year. Marcos goes on a big plane. The plane flies high up in the sky. Circle the picture that shows a plane.

a.   b.

2 A **noun** is a word that names a person, place, or thing. Circle the two nouns in the sentence below:

My grandmother works in the garden.

3 My grandfather is a great cook. He makes good meals that are always tasty. This means that the food he cooks:

a. doesn't taste very good
b. is full of flavor

4 Find a word in Sentence A that sounds like a word in Sentence B. Circle the two words.

A. Karen's grandparents have gray hair.

B. We saw a hare in the garden.

5 Draw a picture of something you like to do with your grandmother or grandfather. Then write one sentence to describe the picture.

_____

_____

_____

Name _____   Date _____

At Home

1 Pablo likes to grow plants. He puts seeds in his garden at home. Circle the picture of Pablo's garden.

a.    b.

2 Rewrite the sentence below correctly. Find one spelling mistake, one missing capital letter, and one missing period.

i rake the leaves four my mom

_____

3 Jose is Rosita's little brother. Jose and Rosita share a bedroom. They have two beds in their room. Jose and Rosita:

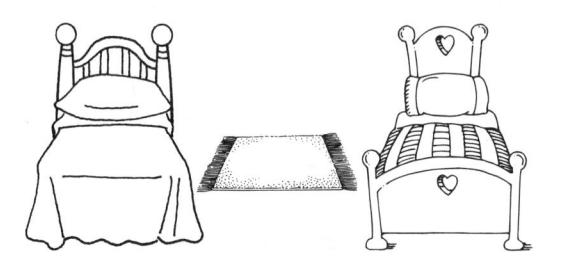

a. sleep in the same room
b. sleep in different rooms

4 Find a word in Sentence A that means the opposite of a word in Sentence B. Circle the two words.

A. The Perez family has a black dog.
B. Their cat's fur is white.

5 Write compound words (words made of two smaller words) for three things you find at home.

bath + tub = bathtub

bed + spread  =   door + mat  =   arm + chair =

_____   _____   _____

29

Name _____   Date _____

In the Kitchen

1 The kitchen is used to prepare and cook food. My parents prepare three meals a day for us. The word *prepare* means:

   a. to eat　　　**b.** to make　　　**c.** to put away

2 "Please be careful. Do not spill your milk on the floor!" cried mom. Another way to write *do not* is:

   a. don't　　　**b.** doesn't

3 Carmen is helping her dad in the kitchen. He makes pancakes and fresh orange juice. She cooks the eggs and bacon. Which meal of the day are they most likely making?

   a. breakfast　　　**b.** lunch　　　**c.** dinner

4 Find a word in Sentence A that has the same meaning as a word in Sentence B. Circle the two words.

   A. The kitchen floor is clean.
   B. The floor was spotless after I scrubbed it.

5 Circle the pictures of two things you would find in a kitchen.

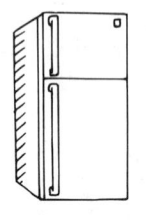

   refrigerator 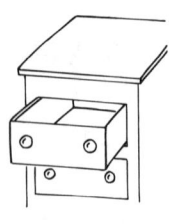　　　dresser 　　　forks 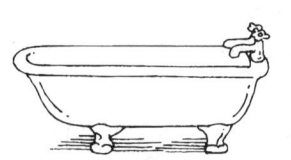　　　bathtub

Name _____ Date _____

In the Bathroom

1 Our bathroom has a shower and a bathtub. Circle two other things you would find in a bathroom.

faucet   toaster   towels

2 A lot of young _____ play with
        childs   children

toys in the bathtub.

3 Joe is in the bathroom getting ready for bed. First, he wets a washcloth. Then he gets the soap. Circle the picture that shows what Joe will do next.

a. put on a bathrobe   **b.** wash his face   **c.** flush the toilet

4 Circle the two words in the sentence that have opposite meanings.

Please empty the trashcan, and then fill the tub with water.

5 Soap is used to wash your face and body. Draw lines to match each bathroom item with what it is used for.

1.   **a.** to clean your teeth

2.   **b.** to brush your hair

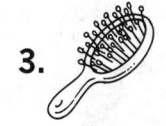

3.   **c.** wash your body

Name _____   Date _____

Clean It Up!

1. Kathy's room is messy. Clothes are on the floor. The bed is not neat. Circle the picture that shows Kathy's messy room.

a.   b.

2. Circle the verb (an action word that tells what someone or something does) in the sentence below:

Jim sweeps the floor with a broom.

3. Millie spilled her milk on the floor. She brings out the mop to clean it up. Circle the picture that shows what Millie will use.

a.   b.

4. Find a word in Sentence A that sounds the same as a word in Sentence B. Circle the two words.

A. A maid helped my mom clean our house.

B. They made me clean the kitchen.

5. Marty likes to keep his room neat. He makes his bed every morning before he goes to school. Circle the picture that shows Marty.

a.   b.

Name _____   Date _____

Time to Eat

1. We eat breakfast in the morning. It is the first meal of the day. Circle two foods you would probably eat for breakfast.

waffles    hamburger    spaghetti    toast

2. An **adjective** is a describing word. An adjective describes a noun (a person, place, or thing). Circle the adjective in the sentence below:

The hungry dog is eating.

3. It is time for lunch. Laura looks at the menu. She orders a bowl of soup and a salad. The waiter brings the food to the table. Where is Laura having lunch?

a. at home
b. at school
c. in a restaurant

4. A **synonym** is a word that has nearly the same meaning as another word. Read the sentence. Then circle the synonym below for the word *piece*.

For dessert, I had a big piece of cake.

a. whole   b. slice

5. My favorite food is lasagna. I like it because I love tomato sauce and cheese.

What is your favorite food? _____

Why do you like it? _____

Name _____   Date _____

Time for Bed

1 Sabrina and her sister, Andrea, have bunk beds. Sabrina sleeps on the top bed, and Andrea sleeps on the bottom bed. Circle the picture that shows bunk beds.

a.

b.

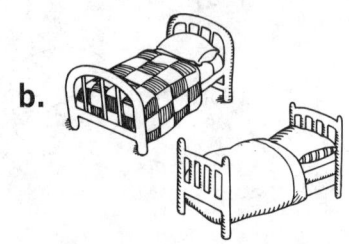

---

2 Armando brushes _____ teeth before bed.
   his   him

_____ also washes his face.
He   Him

---

3 Irena loves to sleep on her bed. It has a soft bedspread and fluffy pillows. Why do you think Irena loves her bed?

a. It is comfortable and cozy.
b. It has too many pillows.

---

4 Jimmy was so sleepy, he went to bed early. Circle the word that is a synonym (a word that has nearly the same meaning as another word) for *sleepy*.

a. awake   b. tired

---

5 Circle the pictures of two things you would find in a bedroom.

sink 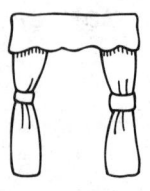   curtains    oven 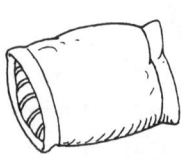   pillow

34

Name _____   Date _____

Manners

1. Jessica has good manners. She always says "please" and "thank you." She is nice to people. Circle the picture that shows Jessica using good manners.

a. Thank you!   b. Give me it!

2. An **adverb** tells how, when, or where an action happens. Circle the adverb that tells how Ralph is going down the slide.

Ralph is carefully going down the slide.

3. Marc was mean to Ginny. He told her to go away. How do you think Ginny feels?

a. cheery   b. unhappy   c. excited

4. **Antonyms** are words that mean the opposite. Polite and rude are antonyms. Complete each sentence with the correct word from the box.

rude   polite

I didn't have a chair. Chris gave me his chair.

He was _____.

I didn't have a chair. Chris laughed.

He was _____.

5. Write the following four words in ABC order on the lines below: respect, polite, manners, please

_____ _____ _____ _____

35

Helping Others

1 Monica is a volunteer at a hospital. A volunteer does things without being paid. Monica visits sick people. She does things for the nurses and doctors. A volunteer is someone who:

   a. helps out   **b.** tells people what to do

2 Sam always _____ to the market with Grandma.
   go   goes

   He _____ the groceries for her.
   carry   carries

3 Julian has a special dog. The dog helps him walk safely across the street. Why does Julian need the dog's help?

   a. Julian is blind.
   b. Julian is deaf.

4 Circle the two antonyms (words that mean the opposite) in the sentence below.

   Lilly pushed the lawnmower while her brother pulled weeds.

5 A **suffix** is a group of letters added to the end of a word. A suffix changes the meaning of the word. The suffix *-ful* means *full of*. The word *thoughtful* means *full of thought for others*.

   Patty mows her neighbor's lawn. Her neighbor thinks Patty is very helpful. This means that Patty:

   a. needs a lot of help
   b. is full of help to give

36

Clothes

1. Mark is going to the park with his family. He is wearing shorts and a T-shirt. It is too hot for pants. Circle the picture that shows shorts.

a.    b.

2. Circle the adjective (a describing word) in the sentence below:

Mara wears short dresses during summer.

3. Candice likes to play sports. She plays tennis and runs at the track. Circle the picture that shows the shoes Candice wears to play sports.

a. 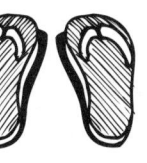   b.    c.

4. Circle the two words in the sentence below that sound the same.

Where is that jacket I want to wear today?

5. Circle the clothes you would wear during winter.

cap    shorts    coat    gloves    swimsuit

Name   Date

Shopping for Clothes

1 A department store is a big store. You can shop for clothing at a department store. You can also shop for furniture and many other things for your home. Circle the picture that shows an item you can buy at a department store.

a.   b.

2 A **singular noun** names only one. A **plural noun** names more than one. Add *s* to the end of most nouns to make them plural.

shirt = one shirt   shirts = more than one shirt

Write the plural form of each of the following nouns.

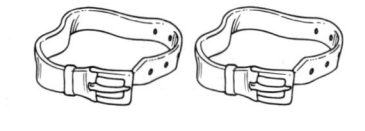

sock _____   shoe _____   belt _____

3 David and Ricky are shopping for their school uniforms. They both get blue pants, white shirts, and blue sweaters. If you wear a uniform to school, that means:

a. you do not dress the same as other students
b. you wear the same clothes as other students

4 Circle the synonym for the word *purchase*.

Trina is shopping for clothes. She wants to purchase a new skirt.

a. to buy   b. to sell   c. to borrow

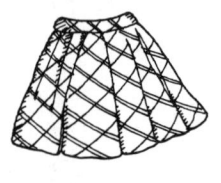

5 List the clothes you are wearing today to complete the sentence below.

Today I am wearing _____

Name _____   Date _____

Fruits and Vegetables

1 Fruits and vegetables are nutritious snacks. They give you energy and help your body stay strong. The word *nutritious* means:

   a. heavy   **b.** healthful   **c.** terrible

2 Circle the complete sentence (a group of words that tells a complete idea).

   a. The vegetables are crunchy.   **b.** Are crunchy vegetables.

3 Melanie cut up lettuce, tomatoes, and onions. She put them in a big bowl. Then she put dressing on it and mixed it all up. What did Melanie make?

   a. vegetable soup    **b.** a salad

4 Find a word in Sentence A that sounds like a word in Sentence B. Circle the two words.

   A. Ashley had berries for dessert.    **B.** The dog buries his bone.

5 Circle the pictures of fruit. Put an X over the pictures of vegetables.

   lemon    grapes    corn    carrot    pear    celery

39

Other Foods

1. Julia's favorite food is spaghetti. Spaghetti is pasta that is shaped into thin noodles. Once cooked, it can be mixed with sauce and meatballs. Circle the picture that shows spaghetti.

a. 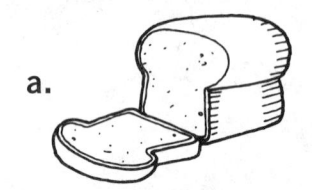   b.

2. It isn't good to eat snacks before dinner. Another way to write *isn't* is:

a. does not   b. am not   c. is not

3. Scott likes to barbecue on his new grill. It is outside in the backyard. When he lights the charcoal, the flames go up high. He cooks chicken, fish, and corn. Circle the picture that shows Scott's grill.

a.    b.

4. My food is too hot to eat.

It needs to _____ a bit.
          warm up   cool down

5. Dessert is eaten at the end of a meal. Dessert is usually something sweet. Circle the pictures of foods that are desserts.

french fries    pie    ice cream    chicken    cookies

Name _____   Date _____

Shopping for Food

1 Mom filled our cart with food at the grocery store. We got fruits, vegetables, bread, and meat for my lunch. What is another word for *food*?

  a. presents   **b.** groceries   **c.** tools

---

2 Circle the complete sentence.

  a. Is my favorite food.
  b. I have crackers in my lunch.

---

3 Trevor wants apple juice. He pays the cashier with a dollar. This means that:

  a. Trevor is buying apple juice.
  b. Trevor gets apple juice for free.

---

4 Circle the correct definition for the word *shop* in this sentence:

  Alba goes to the sandwich shop for lunch.

  a. a place where goods are sold
  b. to look for and buy things

---

5 Marta bought candy and cookies. She also bought a cake. Marta has a sweet tooth. What does it mean to have a *sweet tooth*?

  a. Your teeth taste like candy.
  b. You like to eat sweet things.

Name   Date

Going to a Restaurant

1 Fabian reads the menu at the restaurant. He orders pepperoni pizza. That is his favorite dish. In the sentence above, the word *orders* means:

   a. to make   **b.** to eat   **c.** to ask for

2 Circle the verb in each sentence below.

Marilyn eats Chinese food every day.
She always goes to the same restaurant.

3 The Wolf family is eating at a new restaurant. Mr. Wolf orders the lobster. Mrs. Wolf orders the fresh fish of the day. Daniel and Alex order fried shrimp. What kind of restaurant is it?

   a. a seafood restaurant
   b. a vegetarian restaurant
   c. a steakhouse

Fresh Fish of the Day: Tuna

4 Find a word in Sentence A that sounds the same as a word in Sentence B. Circle the two words.

   A. We always choose a different item from the menu.
   B. Mom chews carefully because the fish has bones in it.

5 What is your favorite restaurant? _____

What do you like to order there? _____

Name _____ Date _____

Our Neighborhood

1 Yasmine lives on a big farm with her family. They have a lot of land with horses, cows, pigs, sheep, and chickens. Yasmine's farm is in:

   a. the city   **b.** the country

2 Circle the noun that names a place in this sentence:

   Frank buys fruit at the market.

3 My Uncle Robert is important in our community. He helps protect our neighborhood. He keeps the streets safe. He drives a black and white car with a flashing light on top. My Uncle Robert is:

   a. a doctor   **b.** a police officer    **c.** a firefighter

4 Circle the two sentences that use the word *block* in the same way.

   a. We have the biggest house on our block.
   b. Marcy played with a block in her class.
   c. There is a market at the end of our block.

5 Next to the pictures, write compound words for two things you would find in a neighborhood.

   drive + way = driveway

   play • walk • side • ground

   _____   _____

43

Name _____   Date _____

Community Helpers

1 A community is where people live. Community helpers improve communities through the work they do. A farmer helps a community by growing food. The word *improve* means:

   a. to make better   **b.** to sell something

---

2 My dentist is an important community helper.

   She takes good care of my _____.
                                    tooth   teeth

---

3 Patty thinks it is important to care for sick people. She wants to work in a hospital when she grows up.

   She wants to be a _____.
                         nurse   veterinarian

---

4 Circle the two words in the sentence below that sound the same.

   Many mail carriers in my neighborhood are male.

---

5 Write the name of each community helper under the correct picture.

   doctor • judge • veterinarian

   _____   _____   _____

44

Name _____   Date _____

Transportation

1. Alex takes the train to work every day. He goes to the train station every morning. The train is long and runs on tracks. Circle the picture of the train.

a.    b.    c.

2. Leslie _____ the bus to school last year. This year she _____ her bike.
    takes   took   ride   rides

3. Lisa is wearing a life vest. She looks out at the water. She waves to other people on the lake.

Lisa is on a _____.
            boat   rocket

4. Find a word in Sentence A that sounds the same as a word in Sentence B. Circle the two words.

A. Mandy rode to the mall with her mom.
B. They drove on a busy road.

5. Transportation is the moving of people or things from one place to another. Some machines travel on land, some in the air, and others on water. Write *land*, *air*, or *water* under each machine.

bicycle   submarine   helicopter   motorcycle   ship

_____   _____   _____   _____   _____

45

Name _____   Date _____

The Airport

1 An airport is a busy place. You find people who travel to many different places. They travel on airplanes. Some even travel on helicopters. The word *travel* means:

   a. to stay in one place   **b.** to take a trip

2 Rewrite the sentence below correctly. Find one spelling mistake, one missing capital letter, and one missing punctuation mark.

   did you see the plane hi in the sky

   _____

3 My dad travels a lot. He flies people in airplanes all over the world. My dad is:

   a. a chef    **b.** a sailor    **c.** a pilot

4 Draw a line from each sentence to the correct meaning for the underlined words.

   1. We flew from Chicago to San Francisco.   **a.** an illness like a bad cold

   2. Charles is sick with the flu.   **b.** traveled in an aircraft

5 A **prefix** is a group of letters added to the beginning of a word. A prefix changes the meaning of the word. The prefix *re-* means *again*. The word *reopen* means to *open again*.

   My suitcase fell open, and I had to repack my clothes. *Repack* means:

   a. pack again   **b.** drop on the floor

46

Name _____   Date _____

The Library

1. A library is a place where you can borrow books. You must remember to take them back on time. If you borrow a book:

   a. you get to keep it
   b. you have to return it
   c. you must buy it

2. Write the plural form (more than one) of each of the following nouns.

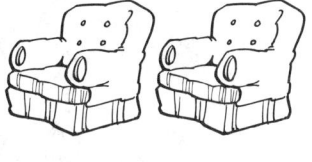

chair    magazine    computer

_____   _____   _____

3. The librarian helps Selena find a book. Selena loves horses. The librarian shows her books about horses. In which section of the library are the books on horses probably found?

   a. Famous People
   b. Machines
   c. Animals

4. You have to pay a fine if your book is late.

   Another word for late is _____.
                                     early   tardy

5. Joel goes to read at the library every day. He is a real bookworm. Being a *bookworm* means that Joel:

   a. works at the library
   b. looks like a worm
   c. loves to read

47

Name _____   Date _____

The Post Office

1 Tammy is sending a letter to her friend, Sally, in Hawaii. Tammy wrote her return address on the envelope. This way, Sally will know where the letter came from. A return address is the address of:

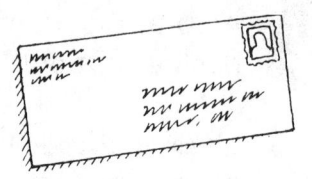

   a. the person receiving the letter   **b.** the person sending the letter

2 Rewrite the sentence below correctly. Find one spelling mistake and two missing capital letters.

   i picked up george's male at the post office.

   _____

3 My parents buy stamps at the post office. We are sending pictures to my grandma. The envelope is big, and it needs two stamps. Circle the picture that shows what is being mailed.

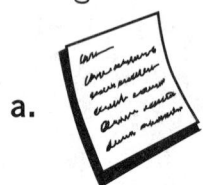

   a.   **b.**   **c.**

4 Circle the synonym for the word *send* in the sentence below.

   My grandmother will send a package to her sister in Texas.

   a. ship   **b.** receive   **c.** pick up

5 The post office gets a lot of mail. Write the names of the three objects below that rhyme with *mail*.

   _____   _____   _____

48

Name _____ Date _____

The Hospital

1 I am visiting my grandmother in the hospital. She will be a patient there for one week. A patient is someone who:

   a. is getting medical help

   b. visits sick people

2 Rewrite the sentences below correctly. Find one missing capital letter and one missing punctuation mark in each sentence.

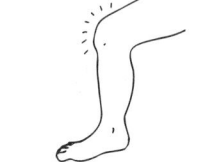

   is your leg broken _____

   will you need a cast _____

3 Gabriel was in a car accident. A van took him to the hospital. The van had lights and a siren. Circle the picture that shows what Gabriel rode in.

   a. an ambulance    **b.** a fire truck    **c.** a police car

4 Find a word in Sentence A that is an antonym for a word in Sentence B. Circle the two words.

   A. Kim's cold made her feel very tired.

   B. She felt lively again after two days.

5 Circle the compound word in each sentence below.

   a. I waited in the hallway to visit my friend.

   b. The nurse gave me medicine for my headache.

49

Name _____   Date _____

The Fire Station

1 An alarm lets the firefighters know there is a fire somewhere. When they hear it, they hurry to put on their heavy pants, coats, and boots. They run to their fire truck. What is an alarm?

   a. a loud bell that warns people of danger
   b. a clock that says when it is time to go home

---

2 Circle the two nouns in the sentence below.

   The firefighter slides down the pole.

---

3 Rex lives at the fire station. When Rex hears the alarm, he barks and jumps up and down. He goes on the fire truck with the firefighters. Who is Rex?

   a. the fire station's cat
   b. the fire station's dog

---

4 Find a word in Sentence A that is a synonym for a word in Sentence B. Circle the two words.

   a. Firefighters hurry to their fire truck.
   b. Firefighters rush to put out the fire.

---

5 The prefix (letters added to the beginning of a word) *un-* means *not*. The word *unhurt* means *not hurt*.

   Playing with matches is unsafe.

   What does the word *unsafe* mean? _____

50

Name   Date

Math Time

1 The **sum** is the answer to an addition problem.
Look at this addition problem:
10 + 3 = 13

Which number is the sum in this problem?

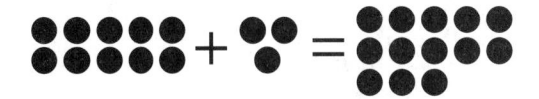

   a. 10   **b.** 3   **c.** 13

---

2 Circle the verb in each sentence below.

Samantha shares her candy with two friends.
She divides nine candies into three groups.

---

3 Rick is doing his math homework. His mom is helping him. She asks, "What is nine minus five?" That is an easy problem for Rick! He tells his mom, "The answer is four." What kind of math problem is Rick working on?

   a. addition   **b.** subtraction   **c.** multiplication

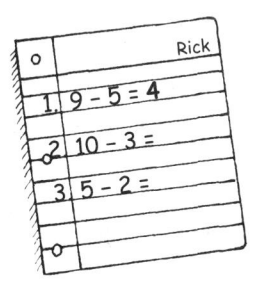

---

4 Find a word in Sentence A that is an antonym for a word in Sentence B. Circle the two words.

   a. The number nine is greater than eight.   **9 > 8**

   b. The number eight is less than nine.   **8 < 9**

---

5 The number 10 is written as *ten*. The number 13 is written as *thirteen*. Draw a line from each number on the left to its word form on the right.

8	fifteen
11	thirty-two
15	twenty
20	eight
32	eleven

51

Shapes

1. A square is a shape with four equal sides. In this sentence, the word *equal* means:

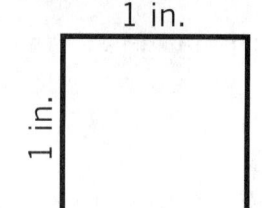

    a. different   **b.** the same   **c.** long

2. Circle the adjective in each sentence that describes shape.

We made round pancakes for breakfast.
We put square pieces of butter on top.

3. Minnie was in the car with her mom. She saw a red sign with eight sides. A shape with eight sides is an **octagon**. Her mom stopped the car when she saw the sign. Circle the picture that shows what kind of sign Minnie saw.

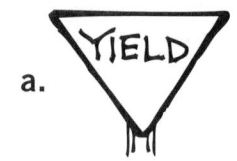

  a. YIELD   **b.** STOP   **c.** ONE WAY

4. Did you _____ that a triangle has three sides and three angles?
              no   know

5. Randy was making a globe for class. His little brother bumped into him. The globe fell on the floor. Randy would have to make another one. He said, "I have to go back to square one!" This means that Randy has to:

  a. start again from the beginning
  b. make one square first

Name _____   Date _____

Money

1 Rebecca earns $5.00 each day she sells lemonade. If she earns enough money, she will buy a new toy. The word *earns* means:

a. to make   **b.** to spend   **c.** to sell

2 Write the plural form of each noun below.

dollar   nickel   dime

_____   _____   _____

3 Roberta received money for her birthday. She wants to save it and put it somewhere safe. She opens a savings account. What is Roberta doing with her money?

a. putting it in the bank
b. buying something

4 Circle the two sentences that use the word *change* in the same way.

a. Kim put all of her change into a piggy bank.

b. Kim gave Steve change for a dollar.

c. Kim has a change of clothes for the party.

5 Write the following four words in ABC order on the lines below:
count, spend, cash, save

_____   _____   _____   _____

53

Name   Date

Measurement

1 **Inches** and **centimeters** are units of measurement found on a ruler. Circle the picture that shows the ruler with the inches. Put an X over the picture of the ruler with centimeters.

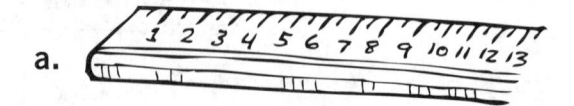

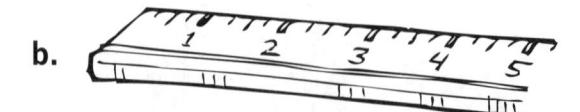

a.   b.

---

2 Rewrite the sentence below correctly. Find one spelling mistake, one missing capital letter, and one missing punctuation mark.

betty bought too gallons of milk at the store

_____

---

3 Carol uses a measuring cup and measuring spoons at her job. She measures flour, milk, and sugar. Circle the picture that shows Carol.

a.   b.

---

4 Circle the correct definition for the word *ruler* in this sentence:

I use a ruler every day in math class.

a. a person who rules   **b.** a tool used for measuring

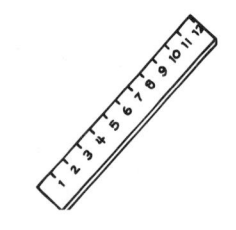

---

5 Draw a line from each measurement to the correct tool used to measure it.

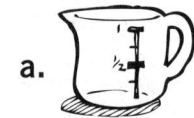

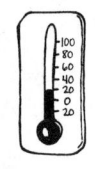

a.   5 pounds   c.

                            2 hours

b.   1 cup   d.

                            10 degrees

54

Name _____ Date _____

Homework

1 Damon has to finish a science assignment for homework. In the sentence above, an *assignment* means:

   a. a game   **b** a project   **c** a test

2 A **contraction** is one word made from two words. An apostrophe (') is put where a letter or letters are left out.

I'll = I + will.

Circle the contraction in the sentence below. Write the two words that make the contraction.

Karen said she'll finish her homework after dinner.

_____   _____

3 Ricky thought his homework was too difficult. Juan helped him do it. Circle two words below that describe Juan.

   a. helpful   **b.** rude   **c.** caring

4 Find a word in Sentence A that sounds the same as a word in Sentence B. Circle the two words.

   A. I will do my homework at my desk.

   B. When is our math project due?

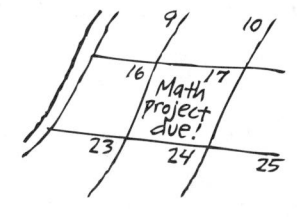

5 The suffix (letters added to the end of a word) *-ly* means *in a certain way*. The word *nicely* means *in a nice way*.

Grace wrote her homework carefully and neatly.
This means that Grace's homework was done:

   a. as fast as possible   **b.** in a careful and neat way

55

Name Date

Computers

1 Carla wrote a story on the computer. She printed it out, but the paper got jammed. It would not come out. The word *jammed* means:

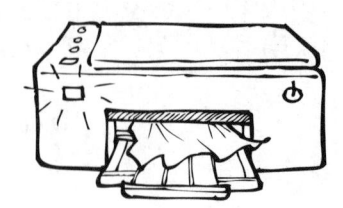

   a. stuck   **b.** free   **c.** open

2 I _____ a new game for my computer.
   buyed   bought

   It _____ me practice addition and subtraction.
   help   helps

3 A computer is a machine. It has a monitor, a keyboard, a tower or desktop case, and a mouse. Which part of the computer do you type with?

   a. the monitor   **b.** the keyboard   **c.** the mouse

4 Draw a line from each sentence to the correct picture.

   1. I pointed to a mouse on the floor.   **a.**

   2. I point and click with the mouse.   **b.**

5 Circle the two compound words below.

   a. mouse   **b.** keyboard   **c.** desktop   **d.** monitor

56

Name _____   Date _____

Time to Play

1. We got new playground equipment. I like the seesaw and the slide, but Ali likes the swings. In the sentence above, the word *equipment* means:

a. things to play on
b. kitchen utensils
c. school supplies

2. Circle the adverb (a word that tells how, when, or where an action happens) in the sentence below.

The children played excitedly during recess.

3. The children play dodge ball. One player throws the ball. The other players have to dodge the ball. If the ball hits you, you are out of the game. To stay in the game, you have to:

a. move away from the ball
b. stand in front of the ball

4. Find a word in Sentence A that is an antonym for a word in Sentence B. Circle the two words.

A. We have to play inside when it rains.
B. It is a lot more fun to play outside.

5. Write compound words under the pictures of three things you might see on a playground.

see • ball • foot • box • sand • saw

_____   _____   _____

Name   Date

A Day at the Beach

1. Randy is a lifeguard at the beach. He watches the people in the water. He makes sure no one drowns. Circle the picture that shows Randy.

a.   b.

2. Circle the two verbs in the sentence below.

Judy swims in the ocean while her brother builds a sand castle.

3. Mandy and her family went to the beach for the day. Mandy's mom told her, "Let me put sunblock on you. I don't want you to burn your skin." Circle the choice that tells what *sunblock* does.

a. makes your skin red
b. protects your skin from the sun

4. Find a word in Sentence A that is a synonym for a word in Sentence B. Circle the two words.

A. The weather at the beach is windy.
B. We enjoy sailing in the breezy weather.

5. I love to go to the beach on a sunny day. Circle three words below that rhyme with *sunny*.

money    run    honey    cloud    bunny

Name _____   Date _____

A Day at the Park

1 My class went on a field trip to a big park. The park ranger told us how important it is to care for the wildlife in the park. He showed us an eagle that was saved. What is wildlife?

  a. the people who work at a park
  b. the playground equipment
  c. the animals in a park

2 If a noun ends in *x*, *sh*, *ch*, or *s*, add *-es* to make it plural.

  one lun<u>ch</u>—two lunch**es**   one di<u>sh</u>—two dish**es**

  Write the plural forms of these nouns.

  sandbox   bench 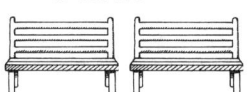   bush

  _____   _____   _____

3 Alan's family was going to the park for the day. They packed up the car with their bats, balls, mitts, running shoes, and hats. They couldn't wait to get there! What are they going to do at the park?

  a. play baseball   **b.** play basketball   **c.** go swimming

4 Circle the correct definition for the word *park* in this sentence:

  My dad had to park the car far away.

  a. a public garden or place to play   **b.** to leave a car in a lot

5 John's family went to the park yesterday. First, they had a picnic. Next, they flew a kite. Last, they went on a hike. Write the words *first*, *next*, and *last* under the correct pictures.

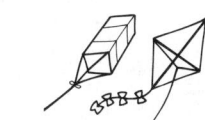

  a. _____   **b.** _____   **c.** _____

59

Name _____ Date _____

A Day at the Pool

1 Isaac does not know how to swim very well. He has to wear a life jacket in the pool so he won't drown. A life jacket:

   a. keeps you warm
   b. helps you float in water

2 Circle three nouns in the sentence below.

   Sophie and her brother play in the pool.

3 Draw a line from each sentence to the correct picture.

   1. Andrew splashes his sister.   a.

   2. Grace dives into the deep end.   b.

4 Find a word in Sentence A that is an antonym of a word in Sentence B. Circle the two words.

   A. The diving board is at the deep end of pool.
   B. Sophie stands in the shallow end of the pool.

5 Circle the things that you can do in a pool. Put an X over the things you cannot do in a pool.

   swim    dive    play soccer    eat

60

Name   Date

A Day at the Fair

1 Vicki always rides the carousel at the fair. It goes round and round many times. She likes to pretend that she's riding a real horse. Circle the picture that shows the carousel.

a.    b. 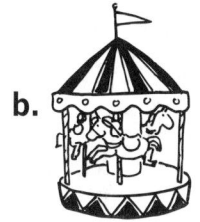   c.

2 Lupe _____ the cotton candy that she _____ at the fair.
      ate   eated   get   got

3 Ben is on the giant roller coaster. It is fast and scary. Ben screams and laughs during the whole ride. He wants to ride it again. How does Ben feel about the roller coaster?

a. He is afraid of it.
b. He thinks it is fun.

4 Find a word in Sentence A that sounds the same as a word in Sentence B. Circle the two words.

A. Tanya rode the carousel five times.

B. The fair was at the end of a long dirt road.

5 Circle three words that rhyme with *fair*.

hair    farm    bear    ear    chair

Name _____ Date _____

Cats

1 My cat, Mars, has black paws. A paw is an animal's foot. He always licks his paw. Circle the picture that shows Mars licking his paw.

a.   b.   c.

2 Circle the adjective in each sentence below.

My dad got us a white kitten. His fur is so fluffy.

3 The cat is lying in the sun. She purrs and stretches. She sleeps all day. The cat is:

a. lazy   **b.** playful   **c.** mean

4 Find a word in Sentence A that is an antonym of a word in Sentence B. Circle the two words.

A. The dog licked me with its smooth tongue.
B. The cat's tongue felt rough like sandpaper.

5 The clouds were dark and gray. The rain would not stop. Mom said, "Wow! It's really raining cats and dogs!" This means that:

a. cats and dogs are falling from the sky
b. it is raining hard

Name _____   Date _____

Dogs

1. Amy wants to train her dog, Oscar, to do tricks. She wants Oscar to learn how to sit, stay, and fetch. In the sentence above, the word *train* means:

   a. a locomotive
   b. to teach
   c. to play with

2. Write the contraction (a word made from two words) for each set of words.

   My parents said _____ get us a dog if _____ good.
                                they will   we are

3. Nicole loves her new dog, Teeny. She carries Teeny everywhere she goes. She has a little bag she puts Teeny in when they go out. Teeny is a:

   a. big dog
   b. little dog

4. Find a word in Sentence A that sounds the same as a word in Sentence B. Circle the two words.

   A. My dog wags his tail when I come home.

   B. Cinderella is a tale with a happy ending.

5. Trina was trying to teach her grandpa how to use the computer. Her grandpa did not understand how to do it. He told her, "You can't teach an old dog new tricks." What does this mean?

   a. Trina's grandpa is a dog.
   b. It is sometimes difficult for older people to learn new things.

63

Name _____ Date _____

Rabbits and Hamsters

1. My hamster is very active at night. He runs all over his cage. He runs on his wheel. He chews on his toys. The word *active* means:

   a. to be sleepy
   b. to be hungry
   c. to have lots of energy

2. Rewrite the sentence below correctly. Find one spelling mistake, two missing capital letters, and one missing punctuation mark.

   we went to by a rabbit at harry's Pet Store

   _____

3. Sally got a rabbit at the pet shop. The clerk told her that rabbits are vegetarians, so she went to buy carrots, lettuce, grapes, and apples for her rabbit. The word *vegetarian* means that rabbits:

   a. eat fruits and vegetables

   b. eat meat

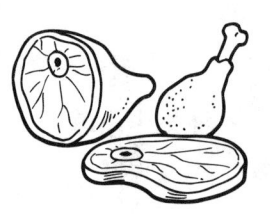

4. Find a word in Sentence A that is an antonym of a word in Sentence B. Circle the two words.

   A. My hamster runs on his wheel all night.

   B. The rabbit is outside during the day.

5. Write the following four words in ABC order on the lines below: rabbit, soft, small, hamster

   _____   _____   _____   _____

64

Name _____   Date _____

Jump Rope

1. Jumping rope is Billy's favorite hobby. He gets a new jump rope every year. He can jump really fast. A hobby is:

a. an activity you enjoy doing
b. an activity you don't like

---

2. Nancy is celebrating _____ birthday.
　　　　　　　　　　　　　she's　　　her

_____ got a new jump rope.
She　　Her

---

3. Peter and Martha are jumping rope on the playground. Other kids are running around the track or playing basketball. The coach blows his whistle to tell them to stop. What class are the kids in?

a. art class　　　**b.** math class　　　**c.** P.E. class

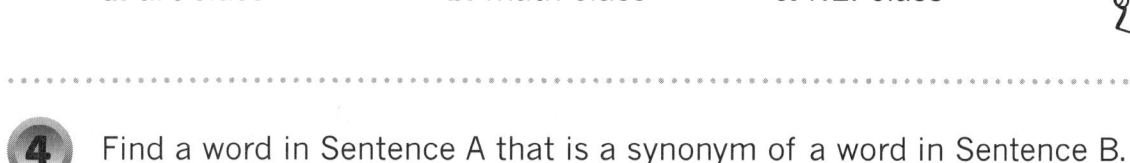

---

4. Find a word in Sentence A that is a synonym of a word in Sentence B. Circle the two words.

A. Myra jumps rope during recess time.

B. Brenda skips rope down the sidewalk after school.

---

5. It is fun to jump rope. Circle three words below that rhyme with *jump*.

nope 　　bump 　　drum　　pump 　　dump

65

Name _____   Date _____

Tag

1 Susie and John are outside playing a game of tag. Susie has to chase John all over the yard. She finally gets him and says "You're it!" The word *chase* means:

a. to run away from
b. to run after
c. to hide from

2 The boys _____ so tired, because they _____ tag all day.
   was   were   played   plays

3 Hank and Harry were at school playing tag. They were running all over the playground. A teacher saw them and told them to stop. They did not listen. They had to go see the principal. What do you think this means?

a. They are getting a reward.
b. They are getting in trouble.

4 Draw a line from each sentence to the correct picture.

1. We got in trouble for playing tag in the store.

a.

2. My pants still have a price tag on them.

b.

5 Tag is a game that most kids play outdoors. It is not safe to play tag inside your house or classroom. Circle three other games you play outdoors.

tetherball 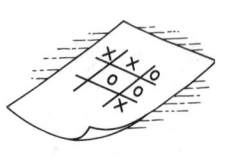   tic-tac-toe    hopscotch 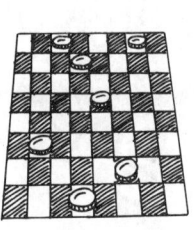   checkers    dodge ball

66

Kickball

1 We play kickball in P.E. class. The pitcher rolls the ball. The kicker kicks it hard. Circle the picture of the kicker.

a.

b.

2 Write the plural form of each of the following nouns below.

base _____   point _____

player _____   team _____

3 Carol was playing kickball during recess. Jerry pitched the ball, and Carol kicked it as hard as she could. It went far! She ran through all the bases. She scored a run! This means that Carol:

a. got a good grade
b. won points for her team
c. lost the game

4 Find a word in Sentence A that is an antonym of a word in Sentence B. Circle the two words.

A. If I catch this ball, we win the game!
B. I sure hope I don't drop it.

5 The boys in my class played kickball against the girls in my class. The boys team tied with the girls team, so nobody won the game! What does this mean?

a. The boys tied up the girls with rope.
b. Each team got the same number of points.

Name   Date

Music

1 Nicky plays the drums in a band. She has to rehearse every day. She wants to get better before her band plays at school. The word *rehearse* means:

  a. to read   b. to practice   c. to watch

2 Circle the two complete sentences below.

  a. Eric is taking guitar lessons.
  b. Really learning fast.
  c. His guitar teacher is nice.

3 Lola plucks the strings on the harp with her fingers. She makes beautiful music as she moves her fingers across the harp's strings. What is a harp?

  a. a musical instrument
  b. a type of radio
  c. bangs

4 Draw a line from each sentence to the correct picture.

  1. A piano has black and white keys.   a.

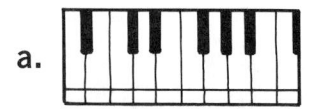

  2. I left my car keys on the table.   b.

5 Sheila had improved her grades in school. When Sheila told her parents that her grades were getting better, they said, "That is music to our ears!" This means that Sheila's parents:

  a. love the way Sheila plays the piano
  b. are happy to hear about Sheila's good grades

Name _____   Date _____

Art

1 Our art teacher shows us how to sketch with a pencil. I sketch a picture of my dad carefully on my paper. The word *sketch* means:

    a. to paint   **b.** to draw   **c.** to color

2 Circle the verb in each sentence below.

Rico drew a picture of his house. Miss Smith taped his artwork to the board.

3 Amy is in art class. She is making a horse for her sister. She looks at a picture of a horse to help her. She takes out the clay and starts molding it into a horse. Circle the picture that shows Amy's art project.

    a.   b.

4 Find a word in Sentence A that is a synonym of a word in Sentence B. Circle the two words.

A. Our teacher displays all of our artwork.
B. He shows it to our parents when they visit.

5 Claudia is painting a picture in art class today. First, she sketches with a pencil. Next, she takes out her paints and brushes. Last, she paints the flower she sketched. Write the words *first*, *next*, and *last* under the correct picture.

a. _____   b. _____   c. _____

Name Date

Dance

1. A ballerina is a dancer. She wears a tutu, tights, and ballet slippers. She puts her hair up with ribbons. Circle the picture that shows the ballerina.

   a. b.

2. Circle the adverb in each sentence below.

   Carlos went dancing yesterday.
   He happily danced to his favorite music.

3. Meredith has dance class today. Meredith loves the tapping sound her shoes make when she dances. Circle the picture that shows what kind of dancer Meredith is.

   a. ballet dancer **b.** tap dancer

4. Circle the correct definition for the word *steps* in the sentence below.

   Peter learned the steps to the dance.

   a. movements in dancing **b.** flat surfaces on stairs

5. Draw lines to match the words that rhyme.

   spin • • two

   kick • • chin

   shoe • • clap

   tap • • brick

Name _____ Date _____

Geography

1 Walter and his family will be driving to Mexico. They didn't know how to get there. Their neighbors gave them directions. In the sentence above, the word *directions* means:

a. instructions on how to find a place
b. lessons on how to drive a car

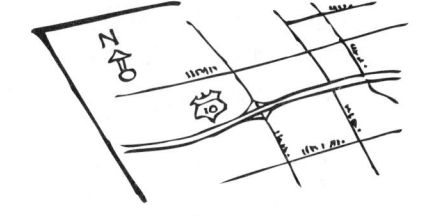

2 Write a contraction for each set of words.

Linda _____ find her state on the map.
         could not

_____ been looking at the wrong map.
  She had

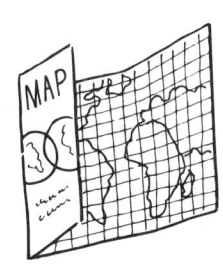

3 My Uncle Walter lived high in the mountains for two years. He told us that the climate up there was much colder and wetter than it is down here. He is glad to live in a warm and dry climate again. The word *climate* means:

a. to climb   b. the weather   c. a house

4 **Homophones** are words that sound the same. They are spelled differently and have different meanings. The words *for* and *four* are homophones. Find a word in Sentence A that is a homophone of a word in Sentence B. Circle the two words.

A. The highest peak in Colorado is Mt. Elbert.

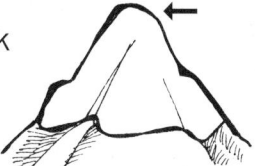

B. Do not peek at your gifts before your birthday.

5 Write a compound word under each picture.

far • fall • sea • away • water • shore

_____   _____   _____

71

Name _____   Date _____

Birthdays

1. Mom's birthday is tomorrow. We are going to decorate the house with a birthday sign, balloons, and flowers. Mom is going to be so excited! In the sentence above, the word *decorate* means:

a. to paint the walls and move the furniture
b. to make something look nicer by adding things to it

---

2. John is _____ his birthday at home this year.
       celebrates   celebrating

Last year, he _____ a party at his grandparents' house.
              had   having

---

3. Lily tore off the wrapping paper and opened the box. She was so happy when she looked inside. Lily said, "Thank you, Tara! This is the stuffed bear I wanted!" What happened?

a. Tara gave Lily a gift.
b. Lily gave Tara a gift.
c. Lily bought a bear

---

4. Find a word in Sentence A that is a homophone (a word that sounds the same as another word but has a different spelling and meaning) of a word in Sentence B. Circle the two words.

A. Bernardo blew out the candles on his cake.
B. The frosting on the cake is white and blue.

---

5. These are things you might see at a birthday party. Label each picture correctly.

cupcakes • hats • presents • piñata

a. _____ **b.** _____ **c.** _____ **d.** _____

Name _____ Date _____

Happy New Year!

1 Carlos wrote his goals for the new year. His most important goal was to learn how to play the guitar. In the sentence above, the word *goal* means:

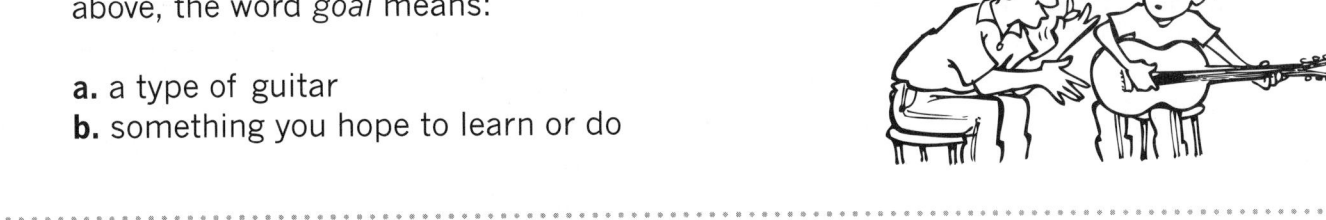

  a. a type of guitar
  b. something you hope to learn or do

2 Circle the correct adjective to complete each sentence below.

  My family had a _____ party for the new year.
                          big   tall

  It was a _____ night.
               fun   sunny

3 Ruth woke up at midnight. She could hear everyone yelling "Happy New Year!" Her mom and dad came in to give her another goodnight kiss. Where is Ruth?

  a. a New Year's party
  b. outside
  c. in bed

4 Find a word in Sentence A that is an antonym of a word in Sentence B. Circle the two words.

  A. I can't believe it is the end of the year!

  B. January is the beginning of the new year.

5 Write a goal of something you want to do or to learn.

  My goal is to _____.

Name   Date

Valentine's Day

1 Marie wrote a poem to give to her grandmother on Valentine's Day. Marie has a lot of affection for her grandmother. Marie likes to show her grandmother how much she cares about her. The word *affection* means:

   a. dislike   **b.** love   **c.** poems

2 Write the plural form of each of the following nouns.

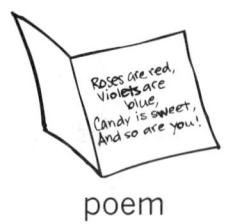

   poem   heart   hug   kiss

   _____   _____   _____   _____

3 First, Andrew made a Valentine's Day card for his friend, Joshua. Next, he put the card in an envelope. Then, he wrote Joshua's address on the envelope. After that, he put a stamp on it. Last, he is going to:

   a. walk to Joshua's   **b.** meet Joshua   **c.** mail the card
   house   at school   to Joshua

4 Find a word in Sentence A that is an antonym of a word in Sentence B. Circle the two words.

   A. My dad gives my mom flowers on Valentine's Day.

   B. Our teacher receives a card from every student.

5 Valentine's Day is celebrated on February 14. It is a celebration of love and friendship. Circle the things you might see on Valentine's day.

   cards   pumpkin   flowers   candy   eggs

Name _____   Date _____

Easter

1 Elizabeth is going to her grandparents' house for Easter. She brings a basket to hold lots of eggs. Her grandparents hide eggs in their yard. Elizabeth and her cousins have to hunt for them. In the sentence above, the word *hunt* means:

a. to look for   **b.** to hide   **c.** to chase animals

2 Circle the two sentences below that are *not* complete.

a. Sweet and chewy jellybeans.
b. Jellybeans are my favorite candy.
c. Buying jellybeans at the store.

3 Jill and her brother, Jacob, are going to get their pictures taken with the Easter Bunny. They wait in a line behind a lot of other children. The Easter Bunny is sitting in a big chair. Jacob sits on his lap, and Jill stands on the side. Circle the picture that shows who they waited in line to see.

a.    **b.**

4 Circle the two sentences below that mean the same thing.

a. Lourdes has a pretty dress on today.
b. Lourdes has a messy dress on today.
c. Lourdes has a lovely dress on today.

5 Easter is a holiday that is in the spring. Circle three words below that rhyme with *spring*.

king    sink    ring 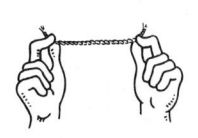   string    spin

75

Name   Date

Fourth of July

1. The BOOM of the fireworks frightened Sherri's dog. He ran under the bed. He was shaking. The word *frightened* means:

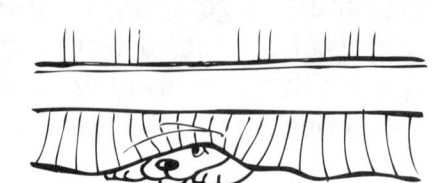

   a. brave   **b.** scared   **c.** sleepy

2. Rewrite the sentence below correctly. Find three missing capital letters and one missing punctuation mark.

   james and alex watch the fireworks on the Fourth of july

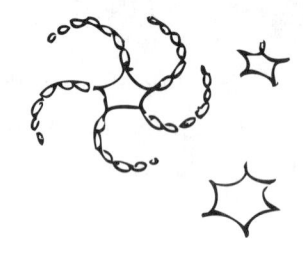

   _____

3. The Fourth of July is a fun day for the Wilsons. Mrs. Wilson sets the table. Mr. Wilson puts salt and pepper on the hamburgers. Jenny and Marissa put out the chips. Circle the picture that shows what the Wilson family is getting ready for.

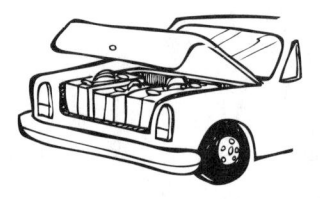

   a. a barbecue   **b.** a trip

4. Find a word in Sentence A that is an antonym of a word in Sentence B. Circle the two words.

   A. The fireworks were bright in the sky.
   B. They looked amazing on such a dark night.

5. Write the following four words in ABC order on the lines below: flag, holiday, fireworks, independence

   _____   _____   _____   _____

76

Name   Date

Halloween

1 Our neighbors decorated their house for Halloween. The house looks dark. It is covered with ghosts, witches, and skeletons. I'm afraid to walk by it. I think it looks creepy! The word *creepy* means:

  a. funny **b.** cute **c.** scary

2 Circle the two nouns in each sentence below.

My dad always passes out candy.
My mom fixes our costumes.

3 Sergio's family got three pumpkins at the pumpkin patch. This year, he gets to carve his own pumpkin. His mom gives him a knife that is not too sharp, so he won't hurt himself. He carves a scary face on his pumpkin. What did Sergio do with his pumpkin?

  a. He made a pumpkin pie with it.
  b. He cut a scary face on it.
  c. He put it on his head to scare other kids.

4 Find a word in Sentence A that is a homophone of a word in Sentence B. Circle the two words.

  A. My sister dressed up as a witch last year. 
  B. Which costume are you going to get?

5 Write the following four words in ABC order on the lines below:
orange, black, ghost, monster

_____   _____   _____   _____

77

Name   Date

Veterans Day

1. Cesar is a veteran. He was a soldier a long time ago. Every Veterans Day, he walks in a parade to honor the men and women who were also soldiers. The word *honor* means:

   a. to walk a long time
   b. to remember and respect

2. Rewrite the sentence below correctly. Find two missing capital letters and two missing punctuation marks.

   veterans day became a holiday on November 11 1919

   _____

3. On Veterans Day, we celebrate the men and women who used to be in the military and who are still living. These people worked hard to guard the United States and to keep its citizens safe. This means that veterans:

   a. protected their country   **b.** harmed their country

4. Circle the correct definition for the word *safe* in the sentence below:

   The soldiers fought to keep our country safe.

   a. a strong box with special locks for keeping money and valuable things
   b. free from danger or harm

5. The suffix *-less* means *without*. The word *careless* means *without care*.

   My grandpa says that he was not scared when he was a young soldier. He was brave and fearless. What does the word *fearless* mean?

   a. full of fear   **b.** without fear   **c.** young

78

Name _____   Date _____

Christmas

1. Christmas is a holiday celebrated by many people all over the world. Families get together for Christmas dinner and give each other gifts. A holiday is:

   a. a day when people celebrate something special
   b. the time of day when everyone eats dinner

2. My grandma _____ cookies every Christmas.
                   bake   bakes

   She _____ them with frosting.
         decorating   decorates

3. Manuel's mom prepares the tamales on Christmas Eve. She cooks them the next night for Christmas dinner. The whole family loves to eat them. Circle the choice that tells when Manuel's mom prepares the tamales.

   a. the day after Christmas
   b. a week before Christmas
   c. the night before Christmas

4. Find a word in Sentence A that is a synonym of a word in Sentence B. Circle the two words.

   A. My brother and I enjoy putting up the lights.

   B. I like to make my own Christmas cards.

5. Write a compound word under each picture.

   fire • deer • nut • rein • cracker • place

   _____   _____   _____

79

Name   Date

Chanukah

1 Avi and David play dreidel every night of Chanukah. David spins the dreidel to see where it stops. It spins for a long time. Circle the picture that shows a dreidel.

a.    b.    c.

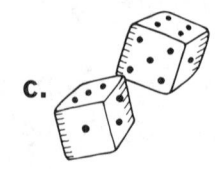

2 Write a contraction for each set of words.

Dad _____ home from work yet. Shanna and Gary _____
         is not   will not

open their Chanukah gifts until he gets home.

3 Chanukah is a Jewish holiday. Families light candles for the eight nights of Chanukah. A menorah holds the eight candles for the eight nights. A special candle in the middle is used to light the other candles. Circle the picture that shows a menorah.

a.    b.    c.

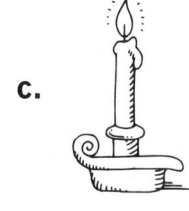

4 "Close your eyes, and I will bring in your holiday gifts!" exclaimed father. Another word for *close* is:

a. shut   b. open   c. outfit

5 Chanukah is a festival of lights. Circle four words below that rhyme with *light*.

night    sit    bite    right 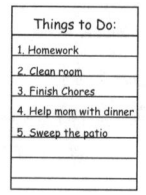   list    write

80

Name _____ Date _____

Kwanzaa

1 Kwanzaa is an African American holiday that celebrates the first fruits of the harvest. During the harvest, fruits, vegetables, and grains are picked and collected from the land. Circle the picture that shows a crop being harvested.

a.   b.

2 The kids helped _____ parents harvest the
       them   their

apples off the tree.

3 Kwanzaa is a special time of the year for many families. They have special gatherings at their homes with their families and friends. Kwanzaa is:

a. a time to spend time alone
b. a time to get together with people

4 Find a word in Sentence A that is a homophone of a word in Sentence B. Circle the two words.

A. The holiday of Kwanzaa lasts for one week.

B. The farmer is tired and weak after a long harvest.

5 During Kwanzaa, families celebrate their African culture, or background. They celebrate by singing, dancing, and having meals together. Think about where your family comes from and a special holiday you celebrate. Complete the sentences.

My family comes from _____.

A special holiday we celebrate is _____.

During this holiday, we _____.

81

Name _____   Date _____

Plants

1 Marla got new plants to put in her house. She got pots and a bag of soil. The soil has important food to help the plants grow. Marla put the soil in the pots, and then she put the plants into the soil. What is soil?

a. a pot   **b.** dirt   **c.** a plant

---

2 Circle the nouns and underline the verb in the sentence below.

All plants need plenty of water, air, and sun.

---

3 There are three parts to a plant—the roots, the stem, and the leaves. The roots bring water to the plant. The stem holds the plant upright. The leaves take in the sunshine. Label the three parts of this plant.

a. _____   **b.** _____

c. _____

---

4 Find a word in Sentence A that is an antonym of a word in Sentence B. Circle the two words.

A. The flowers in the old garden are all dead.

B. We keep our plants alive by taking care of them.

---

5 Plants and animals are the two main categories of living things. Circle the plants. Put an X over the animals.

tree    bat    frog    daisy    snake    cactus

82

Name _____ Date _____

Nonliving Things

1 The word **nonliving** means not living or not alive. Circle four things in this picture that are nonliving.

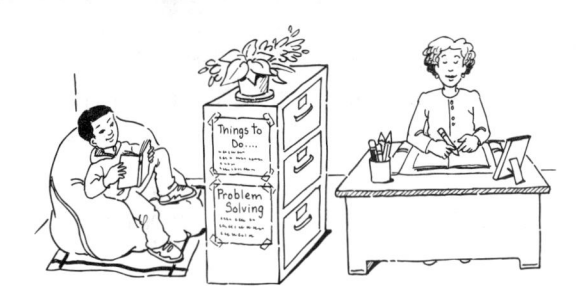

2 Mariana _____ about nonliving things in science class.
    learned   learning

She _____ it was interesting.
    thinked   thought

3 A lion is a living thing. It needs air, water, and food to live. A rock is a nonliving thing. It is not alive, and it does not need air, water, or food. Circle the statement below that is true.

   a. A rock needs water to stay alive.
   b. Lions and rocks breathe in air.
   c. A lion will die if it doesn't eat.

4 Find a word in Sentence A that is a homophone of a word in Sentence B. Circle the two words.

   A. That long board is a nonliving thing.

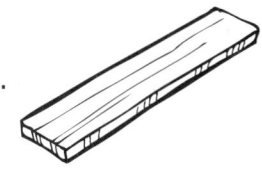

   B. James was bored when he had to stay in for recess.

5 Write a compound word under each picture.

   neck • box • knob • tea • mail • pot • door • lace

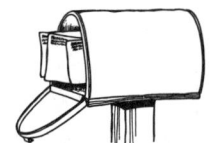

   _____ _____ _____ _____

83

Name _____   Date _____

Habitats

1. A habitat is a place where an animal usually lives. Some animals find shelter in their habitat to keep safe from harm. The word *shelter* means:

   a. danger   **b.** protection   **c.** food

---

2. Circle two complete sentences below.

   a. A fox's shelter is called a den.
   b. Is a good habitat for foxes.
   c. Some foxes live in big cities.

---

3. Coral reefs are warm water habitats that are rich in life. Coral reefs provide shelter for many animals, including different kinds of fish, sea stars, turtles, sea snakes, and jellyfish. What kind of habitats are coral reefs?

   a. desert   **b.** ocean   **c.** mountain

---

4. Circle the correct definition for the word *dry* in the sentence below.

   The desert is a hot and dry habitat.

   a. without water, not wet
   b. to remove water, to make dry

---

5. The suffix *-er* means *one who*. The word *baker* means *one who bakes*.

   The beaver builds dams in rivers. The beaver is a builder.

   The word *builder* means _____.

   The shark swims in the ocean. The shark is a swimmer.

   The word *swimmer* means _____.

84

Name _____ Date _____

Desert Life

1 The **desert** is a sandy and dry place. It gets very little rain or snow. Circle the picture that shows a desert.

a.    b.

2 Rewrite the sentence below correctly. Find one missing capital letter, one spelling mistake, one missing apostrophe ('), and one missing punctuation mark.

i wouldnt want to get lost inn the desert

_____

3 The rattlesnake is hungry. It hunts for its prey. It catches a lizard to eat. Prey is an animal that is:

a. a strong hunter
b. eaten by another animal
c. kept as a pet

4 Find a word in Sentence A that is a synonym of a word in Sentence B. Circle the two words.

A. The desert can get very hot during the day.
B. The sun was scorching when we went to the desert.

5 Circle three things you would see in a desert.

sand    lake    camel    cactus    kitten

85

Name   Date

Ocean Life

1. **Aquatic** animals and plants live in, on, or near the water. Many of them live in or near the salty water of the oceans. Circle the picture that shows an aquatic animal.

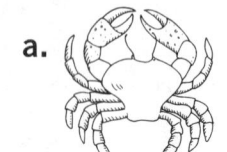

   a.   b.

2. Marta _____ find many pretty seashells today.
         isn't   didn't

   _____ look for more next week.
   She'll   She's

3. Fish live in the ocean. They have scaly skin. Fish breathe with gills. Some mammals live in the ocean. They have fur and breathe with lungs. Circle the mammal. Put an X over the fish.

4. Find a word in Sentence A that is a homophone of a word in Sentence B. Circle the two words.

   A. The tide came in and washed away the sand castle.

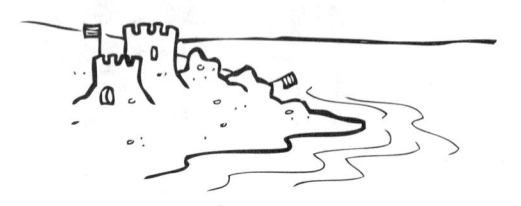

   B. Nelda tied the long laces on her shoe.

5. Write the following four oceans in ABC order on the lines below: Pacific Ocean, Atlantic Ocean, Indian Ocean, Arctic Ocean

   a. _____   b. _____

   c. _____   d. _____

86

Name _____   Date _____

Mountain Life

1. The peak is the highest point on a mountain. Some peaks are covered in snow. Some are covered in trees. Circle the picture that shows the peak of a mountain.

   a.    b.    c.

2. Mount Everest is _____ than any other mountain.
                       taller   tallest

   It is the _____ mountain in the world.
             taller   tallest

3. Desiree camped high in the mountains. It was summer, but she was glad she brought her jacket. Circle the choice that tells what the weather was like.

   a. chilly   **b.** warm

4. Find a word in Sentence A that is a homophone of a word in Sentence B. Circle the two words.

   A. Desiree and her brother saw a bear in the woods.

   B. My bare feet were cold out on the snowy mountain.

5. The prefix *im-* means *not*. The word *imperfect* means *not perfect*.

   Mario and Max looked up at the mountain.
   Mario said, "We can't climb that! It's impossible!"

   What does the word *impossible* mean?

   _____

Name   Date

Rain Forest Life

1 Many different kinds of bats live in the rain forests. They are **nocturnal** animals. They sleep during the day. They search for fruits and plants to eat at night. *Nocturnal* means:

   a. active during the day
   b. active at night
   c. always asleep

2 Circle the two adjectives in the sentence below.

Rainstorms make the plants green and lush in the rain forest.

3 A rain forest has heavy rainfall. It is also very hot. It has more plants and wildlife than anywhere else in the world. Human beings cut down parts of the rain forest every day. This puts much of the plant and animal life at risk. Circle the choice that tells what it means to be at risk.

   a. They are in danger.
   b. They are in a safe place.
   c. They are at home.

4 Find a word in Sentence A that is a homophone of a word in Sentence B. Circle the two words.

   A. Have you ever seen a toucan?

   B. This scene in the movie shows a monkey.

5 Write a compound word under each picture.

rain • net • fall • thunder • fish • storm

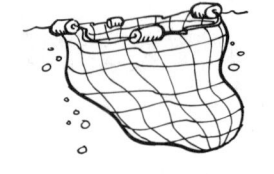

_____   _____   _____

88

Name _____   Date _____

Let's Recycle

1 Pollution is trash that builds up in our habitats or environment. When we recycle or reuse things, it helps to reduce pollution in our environment. Less pollution means that people have a cleaner environment to live in. The word *reduce* means:

a. to make more of
b. to keep the same
c. to make less of

2 Circle the adverb in each sentence below.

Karen neatly collected all the cans and bottles.

She placed the box outside for recycling.

3 We recycle waste material so that it can be used again. Recycled materials include paper, metal, glass, and plastic. Circle the three items below that you can recycle.

soda can    sweater    water jug    newspaper    firewood

4 When we recycle, we help turn a _____ environment
                                      clean   dirty

into a _____ one.
        clean   dirty

5 Too much trash creates pollution. Circle four words below that rhyme with *trash*.

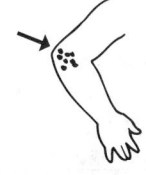

rash    truck    splash    cash    grass 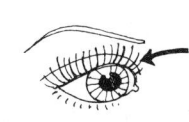   lash

Name _____   Date _____

Endangered Animals

1 Michael is worried about **endangered** animals. Endangered animals are those whose numbers are so low that they might die out. Over 50 animals are on the endangered list. Circle the two pictures that show endangered animals.

a. cheetah    **b.** tiger    **c.** hamster

2 If a noun ends in *x*, *sh*, *ch*, or *s*, add *-es* to make it plural. Write the plural form of each endangered animal.

rhinoceros _____   elephant _____

fox _____   walrus _____

3 Endangered animals are at risk of becoming **extinct**. An extinct animal has died out and no longer exists. Which one of the following animals is extinct?

a. dinosaur    **b.** bat    **c.** dog

4 Find a word in Sentence A that is a synonym of a word in Sentence B. Circle the two words.

A. Endangered animals need our help to survive.
B. Our school provides aid to a wildlife group.

5 The following animals are all endangered. Circle one and complete the sentence about the animal you choose.

crocodile • polar bear • gorilla • panther • panda

I want to help save the _____ because _____

_____

Name _____ Date _____

Our Earth

1 Water covers about 70% of the earth's surface. Land covers the other 30% of the earth's surface. Earth looks mostly blue and brown from outer space. The earth's surface means:

a. the center of the earth

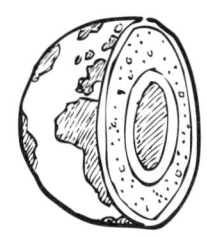

b. the outside of the earth

2 Justin _____ pictures of Earth when he _____ the science museum.
   seen   saw   visits   visited

3 Esther was looking for the United States on a globe. A globe is a model of the earth. A globe is helpful for learning about where things are on the earth. Circle the picture that shows a globe.

a.   b.   c.

4 Find a word in Sentence A that is a synonym of a word in Sentence B. Circle the two words.

A. For many years, scientists didn't know Earth was round.
B. From outer space, planet Earth looks perfectly circular.

5 The suffix -ness means *the state of being*. The word *loudness* means *the state of being loud*.

The earth is surrounded by the darkness of outer space.

The word *darkness* means _____.

91

Name   Date

Weather

1 Dominic is watching the news with his parents. He hears a man on the news say that the forecast for tomorrow is cold and rainy. The next morning, he wakes up to the sound of heavy rain. When you make a forecast, you:

   a. predict what is going to happen
   b. say something that already happened

2 A **possessive noun** shows ownership by a person or thing. An apostrophe (') and an s make a noun possessive.
Example: John**'s** bike = the bike that belongs to John.
Circle the possessive noun in the sentence below.

   Betsy's umbrella has pink flowers on it.

3 Dirk looked out the window. It was the perfect day to fly his new kite. He was able to fly it high in the air all day. What kind of day was it?

   a. snowy   **b.** rainy   **c.** windy

4 Circle the correct definition for the word *leaves* in the sentence below.

   The fall weather turns the leaves yellow and red.

   a. goes away
   b. parts of a plant that grow from stems

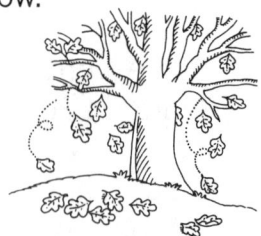

5 Write a compound word under each picture.

   snow • drops • sun • storm • rain • shine

   _____   _____   _____

92

Name _____ Date _____

Electricity

1. Thomas Edison was an American inventor who developed many important tools that make people's lives better. He invented the lightbulb and the movie camera. The word *invented* means:

   a. created   **b.** found   **c.** bought

2. In 1752 Benjamin Franklin _____ that lightning is electricity.
   discover   discovered

3. Electricity is the flow of electrical power or charge. We use electricity every day for heat, light, and power. Circle the items below that use electricity.

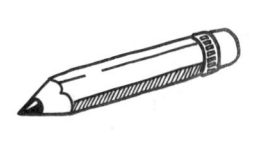

4. Circle the two sentences below that use the word *light* in the same way.

   a. Please turn on the light so I can see.
   b. A feather is very light and soft.
   c. Someone left the bathroom light on.

5. Complete the sentence below.

   Electricity is important because _____

   _____.

Name _____ Date _____

Night Sky

1 The moon looked like a bright **sphere** in the sky. A sphere is a ball–shaped object.

If the moon looks shaped like a sphere, that means it is a _____ moon.

   a. full 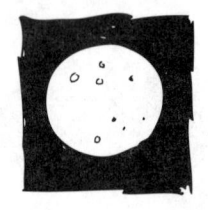   **b.** half    **c.** crescent

2 Linda _____ at the moon and stars last
         looked   looks

night through her telescope.

3 A constellation is a group of stars that makes an imaginary pattern or picture in the sky. Long ago, people used these pictures to help them describe the sky and remember where the stars are located. The Big Dipper is a constellation made from seven stars. It looks like a big spoon with a long handle. Circle the statement below that is true.

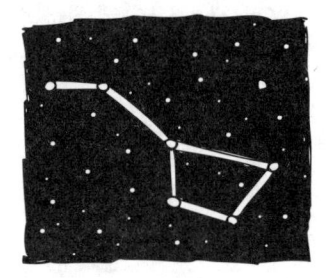

   a. Stars join together to make real pictures in the sky.
   b. All constellations look like spoons with long handles.
   c. Constellations are helpful for finding stars in the sky.

4 On a clear night, the stars are very bright.

An antonym for *bright* is:

   a. shiny   **b.** dull

5 Regina loves to sing and dance. When she grows up, she wants to be a movie star or a television star. She wants everyone to know who she is! She really has stars in her eyes! This means that Regina:

   a. dreams of being famous
   b. likes to look at the stars at night

Dinosaurs

1. The word dinosaur means terrible lizard. But most dinosaurs were not terrible at all. Most dinosaurs, about 65% of them, were **herbivores**. Herbivores are plant-eating animals. They have blunt or flat teeth for grinding food. Circle the picture that shows a dinosaur that is an herbivore.

a.   b.

2. Circle the complete sentence below.

   a. Tyrannosaurus rex was a meat-eating dinosaur.
   b. Learned about Tyrannosaurus rex in a book.

3. Dinosaurs used to be thought of as slow-moving animals. Now scientists believe that some dinosaurs were actually very active. It is too bad they became extinct about 65 million years ago. Write the word in the passage that lets us know that dinosaurs are no longer alive.

_____

4. Find a word in Sentence A that is an antonym of a word in Sentence B. Circle the two words.

   A. Some dinosaurs were thought to be gentle.

   B. The fierce tiger needed to be put in a cage.

5. Jerry was having trouble with his homework on dinosaurs. He got some help from Angela. "Thank you for giving me a hand," Jerry said to Angela. What does *giving me a hand* mean?

   a. asking for help
   b. giving help
   c. giving the answers

95

Name _____ Date _____

Rocks

1. A very old rock sometimes has the print of a plant or animal in it. This print is called a **fossil**. Circle the picture that shows a fossil.

a.

b.

2. Sal is a rock collector. He has the _____ collection
                                                 big   biggest

of rocks in our school.

3. Mom asked Roger to get the rocks out of her vegetable garden. Roger agreed. Two hours later, mom tripped over a pile of rocks on a path next to her vegetable garden. What happened?

   a. Mom saw the rocks.
   b. Mom didn't see the rocks.

4. Sharon lay on the deck of the boat. She felt the boat rock gently back and forth. In this sentence, the word *rock* means:

   a. to move side to side
   b. to shake
   c. a large stone

5. The following words all contain the word *rock*. Circle the word that is not a real word.

   rocking   rockful   rocked

Name _____ Date _____

Life Cycle of a Butterfly

1 A butterfly usually lays 200 to 500 eggs. The caterpillars hatch from the eggs five days later. The word *hatch* means:

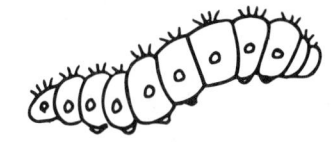

  a. to appear   **b.** to hide

2 Mrs. Morris's class _____ a
           watch   watched   watching

butterfly go through its life cycle last month.

3 There are four stages in the life cycle of a butterfly. The four stages are called the egg, larva, chrysalis, and adult butterfly. Label the four stages of a butterfly's life cycle.

a. _____

b. _____

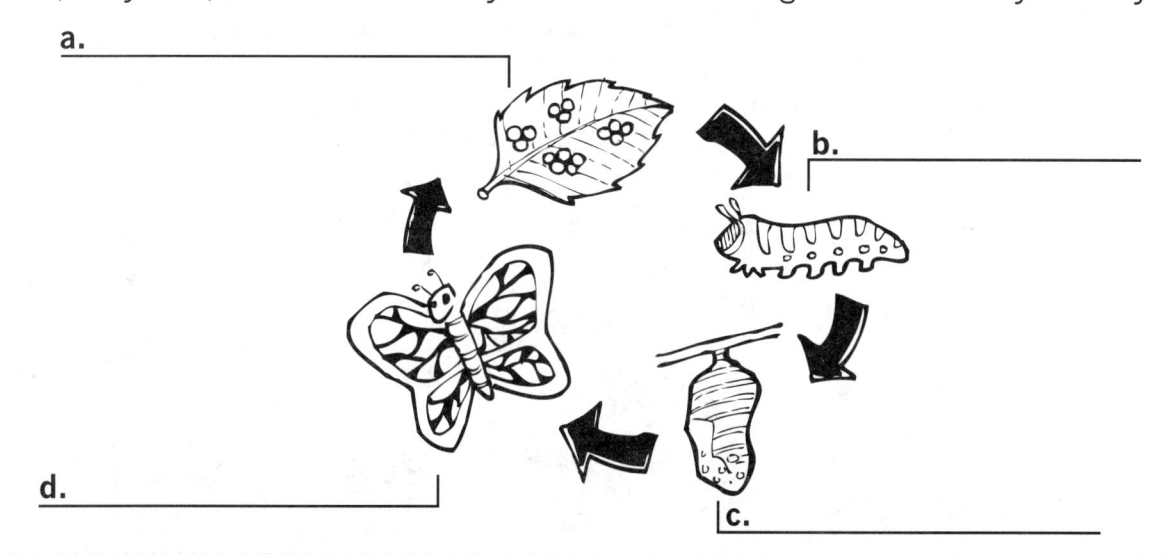

c. _____

d. _____

4 Lisa was so afraid of the caterpillar that her skin became _____.

  a. pail   **b.** pale

5 Draw a butterfly in the box below. Write a sentence to describe it.

_____
_____
_____

Name _____   Date _____

Insects

1 An **insect** has three body parts and six legs. Circle the two pictures that show insects.

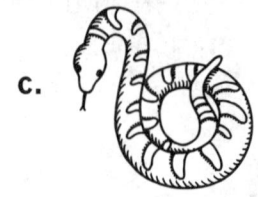

a.   b.   c.

2 The **article** *a* is used before words that begin with a consonant sound. The article *an* is used before words that begin with a vowel sound.

<u>a</u> ladybug • <u>a</u> wasp • <u>an</u> aphid • <u>an</u> earwig

A dragonfly is _____ insect.
                a   an

3 Carlitos has his own ant farm. He also spends hours watching bees and butterflies in his garden. How does Carlitos feel about insects?

a. He likes them.   **b.** He is afraid of them.

4 Draw a line from each sentence to the correct picture.

1. A fly sat on the window.

a.

2. Most insects can fly.

b.

5 Tessa had many things to do yesterday. She was as busy as a bee. What does *busy as a bee* mean?

a. to be very busy or active
b. to have nothing to do

Name _____   Date _____

Spiders

1 Spiders spin webs to catch insects to eat. The insects stick to the sticky threads of the web. A spider's web is:

  a. a resting place for insects
  b. a trap to catch insects

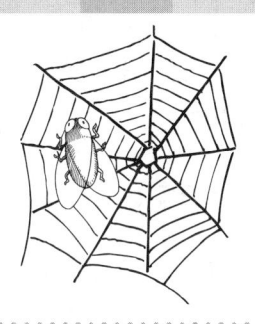

2 Spiders _____ insects, as many people think.
          isn't   aren't

  _____ actually arachnids.
  They're   They've

3 The wolf spider carries her spiderlings on her back. They go everywhere with her, even hunting! It takes weeks before the spiderlings can live on their own. What is true about spiderlings?

  a. They are adult spiders.
  b. They are a spider's food.
  c. They are baby spiders.

4 Many people are afraid of spiders. Another word for *afraid* is:

  a. excited   **b.** terrified   **c.** curious

5 Write the following four words in ABC order on the lines below:
web, spinneret, arachnid, silk

_____   _____   _____   _____

Name _____ Date _____

The Statue of Liberty

1 The Statue of Liberty was a gift from the people of France to the United States. It is a symbol of freedom. What is a symbol?

    a. a test   **b.** a sign   **c.** a song

2 The Statue of Liberty is _____ in New York Harbor.
                                     located   locates

_____ is over 100 years old.
It   It's

3 Edith's grandmother came to the United States over 50 years ago. Her family, and many other immigrants, came into New York Harbor on a ship. They were so excited to see the Statue of Liberty. What is true about Edith's grandmother?

    a. She moved to the United States from another country.
    b. She was born in New York over 50 years ago.

4 Before its 100th birthday, the Statue of Liberty had to be repaired. Years of weather and pollution had weakened it. What is a synonym for *repaired*?

    a. given back   **b.** taken down   **c.** fixed

5 I was playing hide-and-seek with my sister. She was looking for me. I was hiding behind a tree. I stood as still as a statue so she wouldn't see or hear me. What does *still as a statue* mean?

    a. to move around a lot
    b. to not move at all

Name _____ Date _____

Benjamin Franklin

1 Books were very expensive during Benjamin Franklin's time. He wanted people to be able to borrow books. He helped to establish the first public library in 1731. The word *establish* means:

a. to close   b. to create   c. to see

2 Circle the complete sentence below.

a. Benjamin Franklin invented many things in his life.
b. Invented a wood stove called the Franklin stove.

3 Benjamin Franklin is famous for his kite experiment. He tied a metal key to the bottom of the kite string and flew the kite during a thunderstorm. When he touched the metal key, he felt a shock. What did his experiment show?

a. Kites are dangerous toys.
b. Electricity does not exist.
c. Lightning is a form of electricity.

4 Circle the two sentences that use the word *sign* in the same way.

a. He was the oldest person to sign the Constitution of the United States.
b. I saw a sign in the window for the new book about Benjamin Franklin.
c. My mom has to sign my permission slip to the Benjamin Franklin Museum.

5 Benjamin Franklin was an active man who liked to do many different things in his life. When he wanted to publish his own newspaper, he just took the bull by the horns and did it! What does *took the bull by the horns* mean?

a. He grabbed a bull's horns.
b. He took action to make his dream come true.

101

Name _____ Date _____

Abraham Lincoln

1 Abraham Lincoln was first elected president of the United States in 1860. He defeated three other men in the election. The word *elected* means:

   a. selected by vote   **b.** fought   **c.** turned down

---

2 Circle the adjective in each sentence below.

Abraham Lincoln was always a responsible man. People called him "Honest Abe."

---

3 Abraham Lincoln was the 16th president of the United States. During his four years as president, he helped bring an end to slavery. He was reelected president in 1864. Abraham Lincoln:

   a. believed that slavery was a good idea
   b. was a soldier in the Civil War
   c. was chosen as president two times

---

4 Find a word in Sentence A that is a homophone of a word in Sentence B. Circle the two words.

   A. Lincoln was born in a wood cabin in Kentucky.

   B. Young Abe would read whenever he got the chance.

---

5 Draw lines to match the words that rhyme.

   smart •   • corn

   penny •   • peach

   born •   • heart

   speech •   • many

102

Name _____   Date _____

Harriet Tubman

1 Harriet Tubman was a slave as a child. This means that she was owned by another person. If you are a slave, you are:

　a. free　　　　**b.** not free

2 As an adult, Harriet Tubman led many _____ to freedom.
　　　　　　　　　　　　　　　　　　　　slave　　slaves

　She saved _____ from slavery.
　　　　　　　them　　their

3 Harriet Tubman escaped from slavery in 1849. She became a part of the Underground Railroad, which was a group of people who helped slaves escape. She helped 300 slaves escape to freedom, including her own family. What is true about Harriet Tubman?

　a. Her owner told her to leave.
　b. She ran away from her owner.
　c. She took slaves back to their owners.

4 Harriet Tubman was able to guide many slaves to freedom. What is a synonym for *guide*?

　a. to lead　　　　**b.** to follow

5 Draw a line from the words *First*, *Next*, *Then*, and *Last* on the left to the events of Harriet Tubman's life on the right.

　First, •　　　　　　　　　　• she escaped from slavery.

　Next, •　　　　　　　　　　• she led many slaves to freedom.

　Then, •　　　　　　　　　　• she was a slave as a child.

　Last, •　　　　　　　　　　• she joined the Underground Railroad.

Name _____   Date _____

Helen Keller

1 A childhood illness left Helen Keller deaf and blind. Her parents were afraid she was going to die. The word *illness* means:

   a. a game   **b.** a sickness   **c.** a medicine

2 Complete each sentence below with the article *a* or *an*. The article *a* is used before words that begin with a consonant sound. The article *an* is used before words that begin with a vowel sound.

Helen had _____ teacher named Anne.

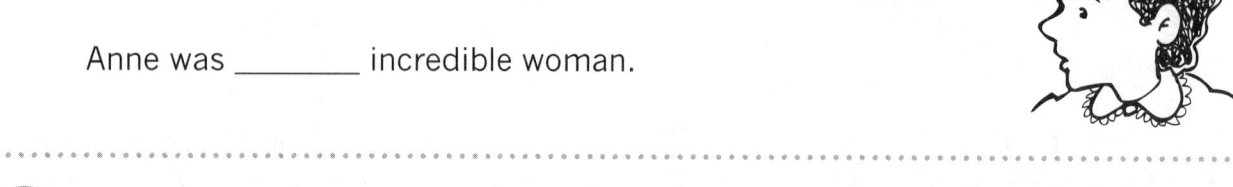

Anne was _____ incredible woman.

3 Anne Sullivan taught Helen how to speak with her hands. She taught Helen words by spelling them out with her fingers. But Helen could not understand what the words meant. After several weeks, Helen could sign many words and understand their meanings. What did Anne teach Helen?

   a. sign language
   b. hand games
   c. finger painting

4 Find a word in Sentence A that is an antonym of a word in Sentence B. Circle the two words.

   A. Helen lost her eyesight and hearing when she was a child.
   B. At first, Anne found it difficult to teach Helen.

5 After many years of learning from Anne, Helen went to college. She was the first deaf and blind woman to graduate from college. She also went on to write many books and travel around the word. Circle three words below that could be used to describe Helen Keller.

   amazing   lazy   strong   talented   boring

Name _____   Date _____

Amelia Earhart

1 Amelia Earhart was a famous aviator. She was the first woman to fly a plane across the Atlantic Ocean. What is an aviator?

   a. a passenger   **b.** a pilot

2 Rewrite the sentence below correctly. Find two missing capital letters, one spelling mistake, and one missing punctuation mark.

did you no that amelia tried to fly around the world

_____

3 Amelia began her flight around the world in 1937. She planned to fly from Miami, Florida, to California by flying around the world. Before Amelia could finish the flight, her plane disappeared. She was never found. What is true about Amelia?

   a. She completed her flight around the world.
   b. The first time she flew a plane was in 1937.
   c. She was never seen again after her plane disappeared.

4 Amelia was the first woman to fly solo across the Atlantic Ocean.

   A synonym for *solo* is:

   a. alone   **b.** together

5 Amelia Earhart visited many countries during her stops between flights. Write a sentence about where you would like to visit.

_____

_____

105

Name _____   Date _____

Sally Ride

1 Sally Ride became an astronaut in 1979. She was the first American woman to orbit Earth when she flew aboard Space Shuttle Challenger. The word *orbit* means:

   a. to jump across
   b. to study
   c. to travel round

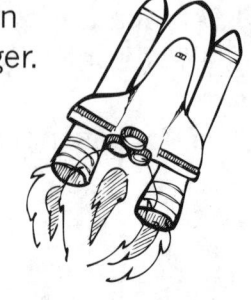

2 Circle the possessive noun (shows ownership by a person or thing) in the sentence below.

   Sally's experience in space was incredible.

3 Sally Ride started her own company called Sally Ride Science. It gets young learners excited about science and math. She especially wants to encourage more girls to study science and math, like she did. Sally Ride believes:

   a. enough girls become scientists already
   b. it is important for more girls to study science and math
   c. only boys should study science and math

4 The earth looks blue and green from a distant view. An antonym for *distant* is:

   a. nearby   **b.** faraway   **c.** behind

5 Before Sally Ride became an astronaut, she studied at Stanford University for many years. She studied the science of physics and even became a doctor of physics! Circle three words below that could be used to describe Sally Ride.

   silly   smart   brave   tired   interesting

106

Answer Key

Hello and Goodbye (Page 7)
1. a
2. is
3. b
4. 1b, 2a
5. Possible answers include: hi, howdy; bye-bye, see you later, so long

The First Day of School (Page 8)
1. a
2. friends
3. a
4. A. happy, B. glad
5. Answers will vary

In My Classroom (Page 9)
1. a
2. Carmen
3. b
4. b
5. block, sock

School Supplies (Page 10)
1. b
2. They
3. a
4. A. write, B. right
5. ruler, paper

People in School (Page 11)
1. a
2. The nurse helps students who are sick.
3. b
4. on
5. Answers will vary.

The Playground (Page 12)
1. b
2. I
3. a
4. a, b
5. Answers will vary.

School Rules (Page 13)
1. b
2. rule
3. a
4. a, c
5. note + book

Colors (Page 14)
1. b, c
2. is
3. b
4. A. red, B. read
5. Answers will vary.

Numbers (Page 15)
1. b.
2. Molly is five years old.
3. a
4. A. to, B. two
5. tree, key

The Days of the Week (Page 16)
1. circle: Wednesday
   X: Sunday
2. My family eats pizza every Friday.
3. P.E.
4. 1. first, 2. last
5. day

The Months of the Year (Page 17)
1. April 9
2. months
3. circle: b
   X: a
4. 1b, 2a
5. Answers will vary.

The Four Seasons (Page 18)
1. Answers will vary.
2. Miguel
3. b
4. a, b
5. snowman, snowball, snowflake

Winter (Page 19)
1. a
2. has, wears
3. a
4. a
5. snowboarding, ice skating

Spring (Page 20)
1. b
2. bunnies
3. b
4. A. scent, B. sent
5. Answers will vary.

Summer (Page 21)
1. b
2. flew
3. a
4. A. burns, B. freezes
5. school, stool

Autumn (Page 22)
1. a
2. b
3. a
4. a, c
5. a—last, b—first, c—next

My Body (Page 23)
1. b
2. runs
3. c
4. a
5. ear, elbow, toes

Staying Healthy (Page 24)
1. b
2. We
3. a
4. A. strong, B. weak
5. hair

The Five Senses (Page 25)
1. b, c
2. a
3. eyes: see; nose: smell; ears: hear
4. b
5. b

Jose's Family (Page 26)
1. a
2. sad
3. b
4. A. son, B. sun
5. rake, steak, lake

Aunts and Uncles (Page 27)
1. aunt, uncle
2. have, plays
3. a

4. aunt, ant
5. aunt, cousin, uncle

Grandparents (Page 28)
1. b
2. grandmother, garden
3. b
4. A. hair, B. hare
5. Answers will vary.

At Home (Page 29)
1. a
2. I rake the leaves <u>for</u> my mom.
3. a
4. A. black, B. white
5. bedspread, doormat, armchair

In the Kitchen (Page 30)
1. b
2. a
3. a
4. A. clean, B. spotless
5. refrigerator, forks

In the Bathroom (Page 31)
1. faucet, towels
2. children
3. b
4. empty, fill
5. 1c, 2a, 3b

Clean It Up! (Page 32)
1. a
2. sweeps
3. a
4. A. maid, B. made
5. b

Time to Eat (Page 33)
1. waffles, toast
2. hungry
3. c
4. b
5. Answers will vary.

Time for Bed (Page 34)
1. a
2. his, He
3. a

4. b
5. curtains, pillow

Manners (Page 35)
1. a
2. carefully
3. b
4. polite, rude
5. manners, please, polite, respect

Helping Others (Page 36)
1. a
2. goes, carries
3. a
4. pushed, pulled
5. b

Clothes (Page 37)
1. b
2. short
3. c
4. Where, wear
5. cap, coat, gloves

Shopping for Clothes (Page 38)
1. a
2. socks, shoes, belts
3. b
4. a
5. Answers will vary.

Fruits and Vegetables (Page 39)
1. b
2. a
3. b
4. A. berries, B. buries
5. circle: lemon, grapes, pear
   X: corn, carrot, celery

Other Foods (Page 40)
1. b
2. c
3. b
4. cool down
5. pie, ice cream, cookies

Shopping for Food (Page 41)
1. b
2. b
3. a

4. a
5. b

Going to a Restaurant (Page 42)
1. c
2. eats, goes
3. a
4. A. choose, B. chews
5. Answers will vary.

Our Neighborhood (Page 43)
1. b
2. market
3. b
4. a, c
5. playground, sidewalk

Community Helpers (Page 44)
1. a
2. teeth
3. nurse
4. mail, male
5. judge, veterinarian, doctor

Transportation (Page 45)
1. b
2. took, rides
3. boat
4. rode, road
5. land: bicycle, motorcycle; air: helicopter; water: submarine, ship

The Airport (Page 46)
1. b
2. <u>Did</u> you see the plane <u>high</u> in the sky<u>?</u>
3. c
4. 1b, 2a
5. a

The Library (Page 47)
1. b
2. chairs, magazines, computers
3. c
4. tardy
5. c

The Post Office (Page 48)
1. b
2. I picked up George's mail at the post office.
3. b
4. a
5. nail, pail, tail

The Hospital (Page 49)
1. a
2. Is your leg broken? Will you need a cast?
3. a
4. A. tired, B. lively
5. a—hallway, b—headache

The Fire Station (Page 50)
1. a
2. firefighter, pole
3. b
4. A. hurry, B. rush
5. not safe

Math Time (Page 51)
1. c
2. shares, divides
3. b
4. A. greater, B. less
5. 8—eight, 11—eleven; 15—fifteen; 20—twenty; 32—thirty-two

Shapes (Page 52)
1. b
2. round, square
3. b
4. know
5. a

Money (Page 53)
1. a
2. dollars, nickels, dimes
3. a
4. a, b
5. cash, count, save, spend

Measurement (Page 54)
1. circle: b
   X: a
2. Betty bought two gallons of milk at the store.
3. a
4. b
5. 5 pounds—c, 2 hours—d, 1 cup—a, 10 degrees—b

Homework (Page 55)
1. b
2. she'll, she will
3. a, c
4. A. do, B. due
5. b

Computers (Page 56)
1. a
2. bought, helps
3. b
4. 1b, 2a
5. b, c

Time to Play (Page 57)
1. a
2. excitedly
3. a
4. A. inside, B. outside
5. seesaw, football, sandbox

A Day at the Beach (Page 58)
1. b
2. swims, builds
3. b
4. A. windy, B. breezy
5. money, honey, bunny

A Day at the Park (Page 59)
1. c
2. sandboxes, benches, bushes
3. a
4. b
5. a—next, b—last, c—first

A Day at the Pool (Page 60)
1. b
2. Sophie, brother, pool
3. 1a, 2b
4. A. deep, B. shallow
5. circle: swim, dive
   X: play soccer, eat

A Day at the Fair (Page 61)
1. b
2. ate, got
3. b
4. A. rode, B. road
5. hair, bear, chair

Cats (Page 62)
1. b
2. white, fluffy
3. a
4. A. smooth, B. rough
5. b

Dogs (Page 63)
1. b
2. they'll, we're
3. b
4. A. tail, B. tale
5. b

Rabbits and Hamsters (Page 64)
1. c
2. We went to buy a rabbit at Harry's Pet Store.
3. a
4. A. night, B. day
5. hamster, rabbit, small, soft

Jump Rope (Page 65)
1. a
2. her, She
3. c
4. A. jumps, B. skips
5. bump, pump, dump

Tag (Page 66)
1. b
2. were, played
3. b
4. 1b, 2a
5. tetherball, hopscotch, dodge ball

Kickball (Page 67)
1. b
2. bases, points, players, teams
3. b
4. A. catch, B. drop
5. b

Music (Page 68)
1. b
2. a, c
3. a
4. 1a, 2b
5. b

Art (Page 69)
1. b
2. drew, taped
3. b
4. A. displays, B. shows
5. a—last, b—first, c—next

Dance (Page 70)
1. a
2. yesterday, happily
3. b
4. a
5. spin/chin, kick/brick, shoe/two, tap/clap

Geography (Page 71)
1. a
2. couldn't, She'd
3. b
4. A. peak, B. peek
5. faraway, seashore, waterfall

Birthdays (Page 72)
1. b
2. celebrating, had
3. a
4. A. blew, B. blue
5. a—presents, b—cupcakes, c—piñata, d—hats

Happy New Year! (Page 73)
1. b
2. big, fun
3. c
4. A. end, B. beginning
5. Answers will vary.

Valentine's Day (Page 74)
1. b
2. poems, hearts, hugs, kisses
3. c
4. A. gives, B. receives
5. cards, flowers, candy

Easter (Page 75)
1. a
2. a, c
3. b
4. a, c
5. king, ring, string

Fourth of July (Page 76)
1. b
2. James and Alex watch the fireworks on the Fourth of July.
3. a
4. A. bright, B. dark
5. fireworks, flag, holiday, independence

Halloween (Page 77)
1. c
2. dad, candy, mom, costumes
3. b
4. A. witch, B. Which
5. black, ghost, monster, orange

Veterans Day (Page 78)
1. b
2. Veterans Day became a holiday on November 11, 1919.
3. a
4. b
5. b

Christmas (Page 79)
1. a
2. bakes, decorates
3. c
4. A. enjoy, B. like
5. fireplace, reindeer, nutcracker

Chanukah (Page 80)
1. b
2. isn't, won't
3. b
4. a
5. night, bite, right, write

Kwanzaa (Page 81)
1. a
2. their
3. b

4. A. week, B. weak
5. Answers will vary.

Plants (Page 82)
1. b
2. Nouns: plants, water, air, sun
   Verb: need
3. a—roots, b—stem, c—leaves
4. A. dead, B. alive
5. Circle: tree, daisy, cactus
   X: bat, frog, snake

Nonliving Things (Page 83)
1. Possible answers: chair, rug, file cabinet, desk, book, pencils
2. learned, thought
3. c
4. A. board, B. bored
5. necklace, teapot, mailbox, doorknob

Habitats (Page 84)
1. b
2. a, c
3. b
4. a
5. one who builds, one who swims

Desert Life (Page 85)
1. a
2. I wouldn't want to get lost in the desert.
3. b
4. A. hot, B. scorching
5. sand, camel, cactus

Ocean Life (Page 86)
1. a
2. didn't, She'll
3. circle: walrus
   X: shark
4. A. tide, B. tied
5. a—Arctic Ocean, b—Atlantic Ocean, c—Indian Ocean, d—Pacific Ocean

Mountain Life (Page 87)
1. b
2. taller, tallest
3. a

4. A. bear, B. bare
5. not possible

Rain Forest Life (Page 88)
1. b
2. green, lush
3. a
4. A. seen, B. scene
5. rainfall, thunderstorm, fishnet

Let's Recycle (Page 89)
1. b
2. neatly, outside
3. soda can, water jug, newspaper
4. dirty, clean
5. rash, splash, cash, lash

Endangered Animals (Page 90)
1. a, b
2. rhinoceroses, elephants, foxes, walruses
3. a
4. A. help, B. aid
5. Answers will vary.

Our Earth (Page 91)
1. b
2. saw, visited
3. c
4. A. round, B. circular
5. the state of being dark

Weather (Page 92)
1. a
2. Betsy's
3. c
4. b
5. snowstorm, sunshine, raindrops

Electricity (Page 93)
1. a
2. discovered
3. radio, TV, computer
4. a, c
5. Answers will vary.

Night Sky (Page 94)
1. a
2. looked
3. c

4. b
5. a

Dinosaurs (Page 95)
1. b
2. a
3. extinct
4. A. gentle, B. fierce
5. b

Rocks (Page 96)
1. b
2. biggest
3. b
4. a
5. rockful

Life Cycle of a Butterfly (Page 97)
1. a
2. watched
3. a—egg, b—larva
   c—chrysalis, d—adult butterfly
4. b
5. Answers will vary.

Insects (Page 98)
1. a, b
2. an
3. a
4. 1b, 2a
5. a

Spiders (Page 99)
1. b
2. aren't, They're
3. c
4. b
5. arachnid, silk, spinneret, web

The Statue of Liberty (Page 100)
1. b
2. located, It
3. a
4. c
5. b

Benjamin Franklin (Page 101)
1. b
2. a
3. c

4. a, c
5. b

Abraham Lincoln (Page 102)
1. a
2. responsible, Honest
3. c
4. A. wood, B. would
5. smart/heart, penny/many, born/corn, speech/peach

Harriet Tubman (Page 103)
1. b
2. slaves, them
3. b
4. a
5. First, she was a slave as a child. Next, she escaped from slavery. Then, she joined the Underground Railroad. Last, she led many slaves to freedom.

Helen Keller (Page 104)
1. b
2. a, an
3. a
4. A. lost, B. found
5. amazing, strong, talented

Amelia Earhart (Page 105)
1. b
2. Did you know that Amelia tried to fly around the world?
3. c
4. a
5. Answers will vary.

Sally Ride (Page 106)
1. c
2. Sally's
3. b
4. a
5. smart, brave, interesting

111

English Language Development Proficiency Criteria

Strategies and Applications for Intermediate ELD Level

English Language Arts Substrand	K-2	3-5
Word Analysis: Decoding and Word Recognition	Recognize sound/symbol relationships and basic word-formation rules in phrases, simple sentences, or simple text. Recognize common abbreviations and simple prefixes and suffixes when attached to known vocabulary.	Recognize some common root words and affixes when attached to known vocabulary. Use knowledge of English morphemes, phonics, and syntax to decode and interpret the meaning of unfamiliar words in text.
Word Analysis: Concepts About Print	Recognize all uppercase and lowercase letters of the alphabet. Identify front and back cover and title page of a book. Follow words left to right and top to bottom on the printed page. Identify letters, words, and sentences by grade one.	
Vocabulary and Concept Development	Demonstrate internalization of English grammar, usage, and word choice by recognizing and correcting errors. Use decoding skills to read more complex words independently. Classify grade-appropriate categories of words. Use more complex vocabulary and sentences to communicate needs and express ideas in a wider variety of social and academic settings. Describe common objects and events in both general and specific language. Apply knowledge of content-related vocabulary to reading.	Demonstrate internalization of English grammar, usage, and word choice by recognizing and correcting errors. Use consistent standard English grammatical forms; however, some rules may not be followed. Use content-related vocabulary in reading.
Reading Comprehension	Ask and answer questions by using phrases or simple sentences.	Ask and answer questions by using phrases or simple sentences. Point out text features, such as title, table of contents, and chapter headings.
Writing: Organization and Focus	Produce independent writing that is understood but may include inconsistent use of standard grammatical forms. Write simple sentences appropriate for core content areas.	Produce independent writing that is understood but may include inconsistent use of standard grammatical forms. Begin to use a variety of genres in writing. Use more complex vocabulary and sentences appropriate for core content areas.
English-Language Conventions: Sentence Structure, Grammar, Punctuation, Capitalization, and Spelling	Produce independent writing that may include some inconsistent use of capitalization, periods, and correct spelling. Use standard word order but may have some inconsistent grammatical forms.	Produce independent writing that may include some inconsistent use of capitalization, periods, and correct spelling. Use standard word order but may have some inconsistent grammatical forms.

*Language proficiency criteria taken from the 2002 California ELD Standards